SCHOLASTIC

Differentiation in Action

Judith Dodge

NEW YORK • TORONTO • LONDON • AUCKLAND • SYDNEY
MEXICO CITY • NEW DELHI • HONG KONG • BUENOS AIRES

Teaching Resources

Acknowledgments

My thanks to:

the researchers and educators, past and present, upon whose shoulders I stand. Their work has influenced and inspired me and deepened my understanding of how we learn and how best we should teach. They include: Lev Vygotsky, Benjamin Bloom, Howard Gardner, William Glasser, Mel Levine, Daniel Goleman, Robert Sylwester, Robert Marzano, Arthur Costa, and Dennis Littky. Others whose influence helped guide my writing include: Richard and Jo Anne Vacca, Rita and Kenneth Dunn, Diane Heacox, Harvey Silver, Richard Strong, and Matthew Perini.

Carol Ann Tomlinson, who inspired me (and so many others) to put into focus the vision of a differentiated classroom. Her thoughtful answers to my questions helped me refine my understanding. Her assistance in identifying research to support differentiation was invaluable. Thanks also to Cindy Stickland for her help.

David Sousa for his important contributions to the application of brain research in our classrooms. He has made brain research more accessible to the practitioner. His review of my work has been a great honor.

my editor, Sarah Longhi, who helped me define the essential themes contained in this book by asking me the right questions. With Sarah, I learned the benefits of a strong partnership between writer and editor.

my husband, Arnie, who fielded dozens of editing questions from me to help me find just the right word or phrase to say what I mean. He provided encouragement along the way and helped me stay focused throughout this project. With unwavering support, he has always been a safe harbor for me.

my children, Michael and Gregory, who helped troubleshoot many technology problems from uncooperative printers to unfamiliar memory keys.

the administrators who continue to support me and help their staff implement differentiated instruction with the goal of bringing success to all students.

the teachers with whom I've had the good fortune to work and learn from, especially those who so graciously shared their own ideas and perspectives by contributing reflections and examples for this book.

the second-grade class who proudly sent me their "Exit Cards" on graphing and followed the process of my writing this book from beginning to end.

all students whose unique talents, interests, and needs motivate us to become better at what we do.

Cover design by Maria Lilja
Interior design by Melinda Belter
Interior illustrations by Brooks Belter and Lily Belter
ISBN: 0-439-65091-7

1 2 3 4 5 6 7 8 9 10 40 13 12 11 10 09 08 07 06

Contents

Foreword

In recent years, two of the major topics of discussion among educators have been: How do we provide differentiated instruction in today's busy and overcrowded classrooms, and how can new discoveries in brain research affect our practice? These seemingly separate issues are very much related. We have known for decades that students learn in many different ways. Some students look for the details, others view the whole picture. Some are better at analyzing, others at creating. Some students work better alone, others work better in groups. Some students like background noise, others want silence. Sensory preferences vary among auditory, visual, and kinesthetic-tactile. And, of course, some learn faster than others. Teachers want all of their students to succeed. But how can one teacher accomplish this goal while trying to address the wide variety of learning styles in the classroom? One way is through differentiated instruction, an approach whereby teachers purposefully plan and deliver instruction that recognizes and addresses learning differences.

Brain research in recent years has made some intriguing discoveries about the workings of the human brain. Some of these findings have important implications for what educators do in schools and classrooms. We understand more about how the brain grows, develops, and learns. We recognize the power that emotions have on learning, memory, and recall. We know much more about the nature of intelligence and the many ways that children can be smart. We realize, too, that today's students are growing up with interactive technology and thus want to be an active participant in their learning. Most important, we know that some of the traditional teaching approaches are not very compatible with the brain of today's students.

Books abound on differentiated instruction and on brain-compatible teaching. But it is rare to find a book that effectively combines suggestions on how to use brain-compatible strategies while differentiating instruction in the classroom. Judith Dodge has written such a book. In *Differentiation in Action*, she has successfully integrated the basic principles of differentiated instruction with activities that translate research on learning into effective practice.

Judy's carefully constructed book starts by reminding us that, despite all the generalities we make about learning styles, each child is unique, and that those unique qualities can make for an enriched and enjoyable learning experience for all. In the ensuing chapters, Judy emphasizes the phases of learning and the importance of giving students choices in selecting from among a variety of learning activities, homework assignments, and assessments. She incorporates the updated revision of Bloom's Taxonomy into the differentiated classroom. Many teachers are familiar with this taxonomy, but Judy's suggestions offer some novel ways to use it to move all students to higher levels of thinking.

Howard Gardner's important work on multiple intelligences is the focus of a chapter that also includes a cleverly designed matrix that combines Gardner's eight intelligences with Bloom's six levels of complexity. Called "Gardner in Bloom," these exercises form a gold mine of interesting, challenging, and varied activities sure to motivate even reluctant learners.

Being a strong believer in the effectiveness of cooperative learning groups, I was particularly interested in Judy's chapter on flexible groupings. She offers useful techniques for setting up many different types of group structures, including small-group instruction, pairing, Jigsaw, and the Socratic Seminar. These varied group formats are useful in implementing tiered lessons, the subject of the final chapter. Although teachers sometimes feel overwhelmed by the potential work involved in tiering lessons, the author carefully lays out the process in a clear, sequential manner that should ease teachers' concerns. Her lists of tips and "how-to's" will help teachers design exciting tiered lessons within reasonable periods of time.

This book will answer many questions that teachers have about differentiated instruction and the related research. In each chapter, the author examines the specific research and the related literature that apply to the chapter's topic. Sprinkled throughout the book are useful guidelines, assessments, rubrics, charts, and sample lessons. I enthusiastically recommend this valuable resource because I am certain it will make it much easier for teachers to plan, organize, and deliver lessons that differentiate instruction and enhance student learning.

by David A. Sousa

Introduction

Why differentiate instruction?

According to Carol Ann Tomlinson, a leading authority on the subject, differentiating instruction means "shaking up" what goes on in the classroom so that students have multiple options for taking in information, making sense of ideas, and expressing what they learn (1999). In such academically responsive classrooms, all students are appropriately challenged and become more successful at accessing, processing, and expressing information. I have written this book to help teachers unpack the complex process involved in running such a classroom.

As schools move from homogeneous, tracked groupings to heterogeneous, mixed-readiness groupings, teachers are asking themselves, "How is it possible for a teacher to recognize and build on the individual talents of *each* student while preparing *all* students for the rigors of new standards and assessments?" This is no easy task. Our challenge is to motivate both the struggling and advanced learners, while, at the same time, making sure that the average learner is equally engaged in quality work.

The often daunting task of reaching all learners can be managed effectively when teachers differentiate the style, content, and process of their instruction. More than just a program or a repertoire of strategies, differentiation embodies the philosophy that *all* students can learn—in their own ways and in their own time. In managing a differentiated classroom, a teacher strives to be flexible and open to new ideas, believing that with new research on how children learn, instruction can be fine-tuned. It is a learning process for the teacher as well as for his or her students—and a highly rewarding one.

The research and strategies presented in *Differentiation in Action* address these key underlying principles of effective instruction in the differentiated classroom:

- Students do not all need to do the same work in the same way.
- Ongoing and frequent assessments serve as checks for understanding throughout the learning process.
- Multiple pathways for integrating information are used.
- Respect for all types of learners is apparent.
- Student-centered activities are encouraged.
- Reducing anxiety is a primary goal.
- Intrinsic motivation is fostered.
- Curriculum should be focused, relevant, thoughtful, and engaging.

- Lessons should be designed around "big ideas."
- Constructivist practices are frequently in evidence.
- Brain research informs instruction.
- Multiple intelligences and learning styles are addressed.
- Multi-modality approaches are enhanced by the frequent and varied use of visual tools and technology.
- Teaching styles and methodologies are frequently varied.
- Choice is often provided to appeal to students' talents, interests, and strengths.
- Flexible grouping is utilized.
- Scaffolding is provided for struggling and English language learners.
- Challenging options are provided for advanced learners.
- Opportunities are provided to help students develop skills as independent, self-directed learners.

A Resource for All Teachers

As I've worked closely with both new and experienced teachers over the past several years, I've come to understand their reluctance and hesitation in implementing a differentiated classroom. New teachers are overwhelmed by the prospect of adding yet another set of ideas to their full plate. Having received little practical support through their education coursework, they need guidelines for getting a differentiated classroom up and running—a step-by-step approach to designing curriculum and instruction. With this book as a guide, a new teacher will come to understand the vision of a differentiated classroom and can begin to implement a differentiated program in his or her classroom. New teachers will especially appreciate the research connections, structured strategies, and examples of differentiated activities from my own classroom and those of the teachers with whom I work.

Many experienced teachers are frustrated by using methods that have worked in the past but no longer seem effective with an increasingly diverse student population. Teachers who are already comfortable with classroom management can turn to any chapter, review the research-based rationale and the description for implementation, and be prepared to engage students in a strategy for differentiation. This book can serve to enrich their repertoire of teaching strategies and to reinvigorate their teaching. It presents research and best-practice ideas that demonstrate how differentiating instruction is a better response to students' learning needs than one-size-fits-all approaches like "skill and drill."

I also hope this book will serve as a resource for student teachers about to enter the classroom. Student teaching presents an opportunity for novices to risk trying something new while receiving the support of a veteran teacher. This book can help prepare student teachers for the reality of what they will face in their own classrooms—diverse learners with varied needs. It will provide them with multiple suggestions for accommodating those needs and the how-to's for carrying out the suggestions.

Teacher study groups can use this book to reflect upon their own present practice. For example, a group might agree to read one chapter at a time and reflect upon the ideas presented and the questions posed in the study guide at the back of the book. They can also conduct action research to see how the suggestions made in the book impact instruction and learning in each of their classrooms.

How to Use This Book

The seven chapters in this book can be read in sequence, or you can choose to jump around a bit. I chose to sequence them in a way that seemed logical to me; but, if there is one thing I have learned from my teaching experience, it's that no two learners are the same, so you may want to approach your reading differently. No matter how you choose to read and use this book, you will find these helpful elements throughout:

- a box at the beginning of each chapter that names the underlying principles of effective instruction explored in those pages;
- an introduction to the chapter that explains why the ideas presented are critical to differentiated instruction;
- a section that reviews the research regarding concepts contained in that chapter;
- ideas for putting the research into action;
- and examples of strategies to help you "see" differentiation in action and adapt the strategies to your own classroom.

In addition, I have peppered this book with reflections from teachers on how differentiation has changed their approaches to teaching and comments about how they have implemented the strategies effectively. At points I've also included a "Things to Consider" section, which highlights questions to ask yourself as you consider the concepts of differentiation in light of your own instruction.

What Can I Learn by Reading This Book?

Chapter 1 presents several learning theories and principles of diversity that should inform classroom instruction, among them: thinking styles, learning styles, multiple intelligences, brain research, and gender-based differences. This chapter will help you recognize and understand why your students are so different from one another.

Chapter 2 offers many suggestions for accommodating student differences at three points during instruction. Here you will find innovative strategies for pre-learning, during-learning, and post-learning that engage different types of learners and have an impact on their ability to retain and use information.

In Chapter 3 you'll find ways to foster intrinsic motivation by inviting student involvement through the use of choice homework, class activities, and projects. Chapter 4 takes student-choice activities one step further, showing you how to develop activities that also evoke complex thinking, as you raise the bar for students. In this chapter you will revisit Bloom's Taxonomy and learn how to weave the taxonomy into your questions, your lessons, and your assessments.

In Chapter 5 you'll discover ways to keep the "fun" in a standards-based curriculum by providing multiple intelligence–based activities. Here you will learn how to tie Gardner's Multiple Intelligences theory to Bloom's Taxonomy and generate complex and rigorous thinking through creative "Gardner in Bloom" activities.

A key element in the differentiated classroom, flexible grouping allows you to vary your instructional approach and choose from a variety of strategies that address the learner as an individual, a partner, a member of a small group, and a part of a larger class community. In Chapter 6 you'll explore ways to maximize student learning and to encourage the participation of all types of learners by varying your grouping strategies and choosing appropriate teaching methods for reaching different goals.

In Chapter 7 we examine the complex strategy of creating a "tiered" lesson to provide appropriate challenge to all students. I place this chapter last because "tiering" requires that you know how to assess student understanding, that you can recognize and create activities that evoke different levels of thinking, and that you can manage flexible instructional groups successfully—concepts that we explore in the preceding chapters.

Finally, I've included a chapter-by-chapter study guide to help you get the most out of the ideas and strategies in this book. Use it on your own or with a group of colleagues.

I have tried to present a balanced approach to teaching, responding to the demands of today's high-stakes educational environment, while at the same time responding to the unique needs, strengths, talents, and sensitivities of all learners. I hope this book gives you the understanding, tools, and confidence you need to meet the needs of your diverse learners.

PRINCIPLES OF EFFECTIVE INSTRUCTION EXPLORED IN THIS CHAPTER:

Multiple pathways to learning

•

Ongoing and frequent assessments

•

Respect for all types of learners

•

Reducing anxiety

•

The use of brain research

•

Learning styles/Multiple modalities

•

Multiple intelligences

•

Varying teaching styles

CHAPTER 1

Celebrating the Unique Talents of All Learners

I wish I knew what I know now when I first began teaching. I struggled through those first years not understanding many of my students, convinced that if they would only do what I asked, they would succeed and enjoy my class. I engaged in a power struggle with Sammie, who resisted my attempts at having her join the rest of the class in whole-group activities. Then there was Paul, who fidgeted in his chair, drawing classmates' attention to his constant need for movement. There was Andrew, who looked sullen and bored even as I tried desperately to actively engage him in what I thought were exciting lessons. Something was not working. I had planned my lessons and thought about the curriculum for hours over the weekend, considering the content, the objectives, and the outcomes I desired. Still, some of my students remained unengaged. A few were even defiant.

As a new teacher, what I hadn't considered was the diverse learning needs of my students due to their different rates of development and learning and life experiences. I hadn't thought enough about their varied levels of interest due to disparities in their talents and dispositions. And I hadn't paid enough attention to their different learning styles. In other words, I had focused on the content and had not focused enough on the *learner.* And so I began my search for information to help me honor the diversity I found among my students.

Over the next several years, I explored many learning theories that informed my teaching and made my instruction more effective for my students. Having abandoned the traditional "one-size-fits-all" teaching methods, I began to incorporate the elements of differentiated instruction into a more effective teaching model—one that reaches all learners.

The Research Supporting Differentiated Instruction

To understand differentiated instruction, I find it useful to begin with a research framework. What follows is a summary of important educational research that supports differentiated instruction along with insights from my own journey to understanding the kind of instruction students need to succeed. I've included questions at the end of each section to help you evaluate how you may already implement differentiated instruction and identify areas in which you'd like to improve. Chapters 2 through 7 provide strategies and examples of ways to put into practice the theories and ideas below.

■ THINKING STYLES

In my own research, I began with an exploration of Anthony Gregorc's theory of thinking styles (1982). His framework for four styles of thinking about the way we view the world (in an abstract or concrete way) and the way we order the world (in a sequential or random order) helped me understand that the students in front of me were as different from each other as

Figure 1.1

ADDRESSING DIFFERENT THINKING STYLES

Concrete random thinkers	are creative divergent thinkers, make intuitive leaps, enjoy unstructured problem-solving, like choices, self-motivate, see the big picture not the details.
Concrete sequential thinkers	like order, respond to step-by-step instruction, enjoy learning through concrete materials, attend to details, work with a timeline, and appreciate structure.
Abstract random thinkers	are guided by emotion and interest, seek environments that are active, busy, and unstructured, and like to discuss ideas and interact with others.
Abstract sequential thinkers	enjoy theory and abstract thought, focus on knowledge and facts, thrive on independent investigation and research, and usually prefer to work alone to prove things for themselves.

(Gregorc, 1982)

TIP

We must first recognize that the way we learned the information we plan to teach is not necessarily the way our students will learn it. The challenge is to stretch beyond our own comfort zones in teaching style and provide choice and options for students who do not learn the same way we do. Gayle Gregory and Carolyn Chapman (2002) use a powerful metaphor of "baiting" the hook with what the fish like, not what the fisherman likes, suggesting that teachers seek teaching and learning strategies that appeal to their students, not necessarily to themselves. Ultimately, the way we teach must extend beyond our own preferences and beyond the way we remember being taught.

they were from me. Figure 1.1 lists some characteristics that describe each of the four thinking styles.

I recognized myself in Gregorc's description of a learner who likes order, step-by-step instruction, and lots of structure—a concrete sequential thinker. But, I also recognized that many of my students were different. For example, Ryan was pretty much my "thinking" opposite. He was an abstract random thinker, guided by emotion, who enjoyed busy, unstructured time. He favored working with peers and having lots of freedom and interaction. In contrast, Christina preferred to work on her own and enjoyed theory, abstract thought, and independent research: She was an abstract sequential thinker.

As I took the time to recognize these differences, I realized I could no longer teach without addressing them in my lessons. I began to offer choices in the way students could work (alone or with peers). I provided written timelines for long-term assignments while offering the option for a more independent student to present me with his or her own contract or agenda for the project. I made sure that some parts of my lessons accommodated my students who needed a quiet environment to process information and that other parts of my lessons were busy, interactive, and less structured.

How well do your lessons address your students' different thinking styles? When addressing diverse thinking styles in your classroom, you'll probably need to make a conscious effort to balance the usual structure and format of your instruction—likely a reflection of your own thinking style—with activities and procedures that will appeal to other "thinkers" in your classroom. Use the checklist below to identify areas in which you might adjust your instruction.

Things to Consider: Thinking Styles

Have I

❍ included a balance of structure and freedom to accommodate different thinking styles?

❍ provided timelines, deadlines, and guidance for students who require structure, while at the same time allowing flexibility for more independent students?

❍ insisted that students always work in pairs or groups or have I offered them the option of working alone?

❍ made sure that *sometimes* the learning environment is active, busy, and unstructured?

❍ made sure that at other times the learning environment is quiet, unhurried, and structured?

■ FOUR LEARNING STYLES

Cognitive diversity accounts for differences in the ways people take in information, use that information, and interact with others. Silver and his colleagues identified *four learning styles* based on the work of Carl Jung and Isabel Briggs Meyers (Silver, Hanson, Strong, Schwartz, 1980).

The *Mastery Style* describes learning that focuses on remembering basic facts and details. Students who prefer this style or possess this strength learn best through procedures. They like to perform calculations and computations in math. They enjoy learning through observation, memorizing, practicing, and sequencing. The *Understanding Style* describes learning that develops reasoning skills and an understanding of concepts, patterns, and proofs for ideas. Students who prefer this style learn best conceptually. They use higher-level thinking skills to compare and contrast, analyze and summarize, establish cause and effect, and support or refute ideas. They like to use reason, explain why things happen, suggest rules, and identify patterns. The *Interpersonal Style* describes learning from approaches that emphasize cooperative learning, real-life contexts, and connections to everyday life. Students who prefer this style learn best contextually. They enjoy giving personal responses. Through interaction with others, they take in information, personalize and prioritize it, and then share it with others. The *Self-Expressive Style* describes learning that produces original work using creative application and synthesis of old skills and information. Students who prefer this style are divergent thinkers who learn best through investigation. They like to use information in new ways, visualizing and creating images, solving problems, and generating metaphors for their new understandings.

To help all students experience success in the classroom, the authors recommend the teaching of content through a rotation of all four learning styles (see Figure 1.2).

This "task rotation" can be used while students are engaged in an activity to help them make sense of the information or afterward to help them synthesize and reflect upon what they've studied. (See Chapter 2 for ways to differentiate instruction through the three stages of learning: before, during, and after.) Students rotate through tasks that emphasize each of the four styles of learning. This allows them to use their preferred learning style(s) and to strengthen less-preferred styles. Alternatively, you can give students a choice of one or two tasks and then bring the class together to share the different products students have created. Keep in mind that although a student may prefer one style, he or she will attain deeper understanding of topics and concepts when you encourage him or her to use other learning styles—"stretching" the student beyond his or her comfort zone. Figure 1.3 shows a task rotation developed for a unit on nutrition that offers students many activity choices.

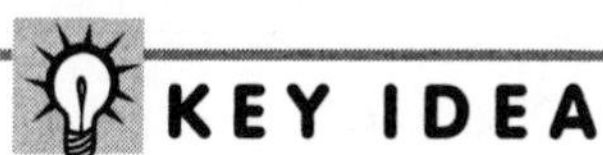

Allow students to use their preferred learning style at times in order for them to feel most comfortable in your classroom. At other times, encourage students to stretch beyond their comfort zones and use other styles. This will help them gain deeper understanding and multiple perspectives of the material studied.

Figure 1.2

MASTERY STYLE
Recall

Provide strategies that require students to remember facts or definitions, use sequences, and create categories and/or procedures.

INTERPERSONAL STYLE
Relate personally

Provide strategies that invite students to converse, deepen personal relationships, explore feelings, and express preferences and value judgments.

Rotate Your Teaching of Content Through Four Learning Styles

SELF-EXPRESSIVE STYLE
Reorganize

Provide strategies that emphasize visualization and imagination, and challenge students to hypothesize, wonder, elaborate, use metaphors, and/or solve problems.

UNDERSTANDING STYLE
Reason

Provide strategies that encourage students to develop critical and analytical thinking by comparing and contrasting, summarizing, establishing cause and effect, proving hunches, and identifying patterns, concepts, and proofs.

(Adapted from Silver et al., 1980; Silver, Strong, & Perini, 2000; Strong, Thomas, Perini, & Silver, 2004)

Things to Consider: Four Learning Styles

Have I provided learning opportunities for my students

❍ to acquire knowledge and skills through drill, memorization, repetition, practice, and application?

❍ to acquire knowledge and skills through personal sharing of feelings and judgments, individual and social awareness, and collaborative group work?

❍ to think, reason, and defend their conclusions through observing and describing data, comparing and contrasting, and identifying patterns and concepts?

❍ to acquire knowledge and skills through creative and divergent thinking, visualization and imagination, problem-solving, and metaphorical thinking?

Figure 1.3 shows how a group of fifth-grade teachers and I developed a task rotation on the topic of nutrition. We provided several options within each style. (When introducing this strategy, you might want to simplify the process by providing only one task for each learning style.)

Figure 1.3

Creating a Task Rotation

NUTRITION UNIT

Mastery Task

- List the food groups.
- Looking at food labels, order the foods according to fat content, carbohydrate content, and calories.
- Draw the current model of the food pyramid.
- Draw a graph to illustrate the percentages of fat and sugar in your favorite food.
- Given three boxes of cereal, determine the amounts of sugar, fat, and calories in each. Record which has the least/most of each element.

Interpersonal Task

- Advise a family member about better choices for a healthy lifestyle.
- Survey your peers for healthy menu suggestions for the cafeteria.
- Interview the school nurse about components of a healthy diet or effects of an unhealthy diet.
- Debate for or against vending machines in the school cafeteria.

Self-Expressive Task

- Create a healthy snack that doesn't exist today.
- Create a month of healthy lunch choices for the cafeteria to serve.
- Write a song to advertise at least four components of a healthy lifestyle.
- Create a healthy menu for a famous historical figure or fictional character.

Understanding Task

- Describe the effects of an unhealthy diet.
- Describe a healthy meal. Explain your choices.
- Compare and contrast the old and new food pyramids.
- Compare and contrast your lunch and a friend's lunch with regards to the fat, sugar, and calorie content.
- Using a menu from a fast food restaurant, choose a meal for a healthy lunch and one for an unhealthy lunch. Explain your reasoning.

(Developed with Mineola Teachers)

■ SENSORY APPROACHES TO LEARNING

In 1987 Rita and Ken Dunn proposed a different model. Their research led them to classify learning styles as auditory, visual, tactile, and kinesthetic. They found that while some children responded best to spoken and other auditory cues (auditory learners), other students learned best with cues provided in written or pictorial form (visual learners). Still others

TIP

It's important to note that while children do have learning preferences with regards to modalities (styles), research shows that teaching all content in their best modality does not equal greater achievement. The content's best modality is more important for achievement (Willingham, 2005).

For example, if you want students to learn and remember what something looks like, then your presentation should be visual. Orally describing the Roman Coliseum to students is not as effective as showing them a picture or model of it. Likewise, having students read about 1920s Ragtime music would not be as effective as listening to a CD of Scott Joplin playing his famous rags.

CONTINUED

needed to handle concrete materials like tiles, letters, or computer keyboards (tactile learners) or engage in physical activity or movement (kinesthetic learners).

By creating different activities for each of these different learning styles, I found it easy to address some of the diversity among my students—and reengage them. I made sure to include listening centers and directions on tape for my auditory learners. For my visual learners, I frequently wrote on the board with colored chalk and provided colored pencils for students to mark their notebooks in a variety of ways (boxes around key ideas, circles around causes and effects, lines under important vocabulary terms). We color-coded exemplar compositions by identifying introductions, key ideas, details, transitions, and conclusions, providing an *aha!* moment for those who previously couldn't "see" what logical and coherent writing looked like. My tactile learners benefited from use of all types of manipulatives (including flashcards, tangrams, sentence strips, and sticky notes) and any tools or equipment they could touch and handle. My kinesthetic learners stopped falling out of chairs and fidgeting when I made sure to include task rotations, small-group activities, simulations, and activities at the dry-erase board in my lessons.

Which style best describes your teaching? Take a moment to identify your preferred style and those of the students with whom you experience the greatest challenge—they may have preferred learning styles that are very different from yours and that may not be addressed by your instructional style. Use the chart below to help you identify the learning styles that you may need to address more fully.

Things to Consider: Sensory Approaches to Learning

Have I planned to accommodate different learning styles with a variety of learning activities such as:

❍ activities that involve spoken and heard material: discussions, paired readings, conversations, oral reports, recordings, listening centers, think-pair-share, partnerships? (auditory learners)

❍ activities that include information that can be seen or read: graphic organizers, summaries, use of color and highlighters, note-taking, pictures, diagrams, illustrations, photos, video? (visual learners)

❍ activities that allow students to handle and manipulate materials: making displays, writing, drawing, using manipulatives, equipment, tools? (tactile learners)

❍ activities that allow students to do and move and become physically involved: construction activities, simulations, role plays? (kinesthetic learners)

(Based on the work of Dunn & Dunn, 1987)

■ MULTIPLE INTELLIGENCES

By the early 1990s psychologist Howard Gardner's research on multiple intelligences had reached our educational circles. His theory helped us realize that anything important enough to learn could and probably should be taught in more than one way. In addition to the ways we had traditionally thought of student intelligence (as strengths in either verbal-linguistic or logical-mathematical areas—the areas "tested" in school), Gardner introduced us to other intelligences. This broadened our concept of how we and our students are "smart."

Gardner identified an *interpersonal intelligence*, characterized by the ability to communicate well, to be a leader, to feel empathy, and to enjoy working with others. He also showed us that some people have a *musical intelligence*, which enables them to learn to play an instrument or sing, be sensitive to noise and sounds, recognize patterns (as in poetry), or have a developed sense of rhythm. Further, he designated an *intrapersonal intelligence*, through which an individual knows him- or herself well, sets personal goals, and enjoys being alone and engaging in personal hobbies. Gardner identified a *spatial intelligence* in individuals who possess a strong inclination to represent ideas graphically, create mental images, notice visual details, and draw and sketch. He also named a *bodily-kinesthetic intelligence*, through which an individual has a propensity for movement, excelling in activities requiring strength, agility, speed, or eye-hand coordination. In addition, he identified a *naturalist intelligence*, denoted by an individual's ability to find patterns in nature, concern for plants and animals as well as ecological issues, and strong desire to work in natural settings.

Coming on the heels of Gregorc's thinking-styles research and bolstered by the learning styles models of Silver et al. and Dunn & Dunn, multiple intelligences theory seriously challenged the notion that all students receive an equal opportunity to learn in a traditional, teacher-centered classroom with largely auditory instruction and pencil-and-paper exercises. My colleagues and I began to understand that *variety* is the key to reaching all students. We needed to introduce information using strategies that appealed to all these intelligences and then provide multiple ways for students to internalize the information. Finally, we needed to create assorted opportunities for students to demonstrate their knowledge. A multiple-intelligences movement in education was born that strengthened the call for varied teaching strategies and multiple assessments, a call for *differentiation* in our classrooms.

In response, I began to integrate multiple intelligence–based activities in class work and homework. Instead of one research paper assignment, I provided students with a choice of several project options and I worked to create different types of assessments that helped students show what they'd learned in ways that allowed them to capitalize on their intelligences,

TIP CONTINUED

So does this new cognitive research mean you shouldn't bother teaching to a child's preferred learning style? I would argue that teaching to a child's strength makes him or her feel comfortable in the classroom and this translates into greater motivation on the part of that student. Without motivation, students achieve little. So, by doing both, paying attention to the content's best modality and, at times, addressing the student's preferred learning style, you can set the stage for even greater achievement.

Variety is a key to reaching all students.

such as student-written plays or model-building. Toward the end of a lesson, I would give students the option of summarizing their learning by making a sketch (for visual learners), by designing a graphic organizer (for logical-mathematical learners), or by discussing with a partner the key ideas and preparing and presenting to the class a summary using an overhead transparency (for interpersonal learners). Occasionally, a few students would opt to create a song or rap that synthesized the key concepts of the topic (musical learners).

The questions below can help you assess your instructional preferences and plan for instruction with multiple intelligence–based activities throughout the stages of learning. (See Chapter 5 for strategies to differentiate instruction guided by multiple intelligences theory and Chapter 2 for ways to differentiate instruction through all stages of learning.)

Things to Consider: Multiple Intelligences

Have I integrated multiple intelligence–based activities in my lessons to help students acquire content (before learning), process information (during learning), and demonstrate understanding (after learning)?

❍ ***Before learning:*** Have I engaged several intelligences while presenting information to the class? For example, have I

- provided materials for discovery and manipulation? (*bodily-kinesthetic*)
- presented an oral story with new information in context? (*auditory*)
- introduced terms in a graphic organizer on the blackboard? (*logical-mathematical*)

❍ ***During learning:*** Have I encouraged students to use several intelligences to make sense of the information? For example, have I provided opportunities for students to

- complete a freewrite on the topic? (*verbal-linguistic*)
- turn to a partner and discuss? (*interpersonal*)
- draw a diagram to make the information memorable? (*spatial*)

❍ ***After learning:*** Have I allowed students to choose from among numerous multiple intelligence–based activities to demonstrate knowledge and understanding of the topic? For example, have I provided opportunities for students to

- write journal entries from a particular point of view? (*intrapersonal*)
- role-play a pivotal scene or possible scenario? (*bodily-kinesthetic*)
- write a children's book about the topic? (*verbal-linguistic*)

■ UNIQUE MINDS AND LEARNING DIFFERENCES

In 1995 cognitive researcher Robert Sylwester suggested that learners have "designer brains" (1995). The unique circuitry in each of our brains is the reason why we each have distinct preferences about where, when, and how we learn. Dramatic advances in brain research have provided strong support for a differentiated approach to teaching and learning. Considering the significant findings about how the brain learns, it is now no surprise that a one-size-fits-all approach does not work in most classrooms. When our instruction accommodates the way a learner prefers to work, the results are often different from those we find when we impose a certain learning environment or activity.

Many students will act out if they are in an environment that is extremely uncomfortable for them. Others will become extraordinarily passive. We all have seen fidgety students who are required to sit and work at their desks for the duration of the school day. We have seen students with glazed eyes trying to sustain attention during a 30-minute lecture. Research about how the brain learns suggests that if we provide some type of movement for the first group of students (getting up to write on the board, turning to talk and summarize with partners) and an additional mode of instruction for the second group of students (vivid posters, interesting videos, appropriate artifacts), we can expect students to be more engaged.

Dr. Mel Levine, professor of pediatrics at the University of North Carolina's medical school and cofounder of All Kinds of Minds, a nonprofit institute for the study of differences in learning, offers hope to all kinds of learners. In his groundbreaking framework for student success, Levine identified eight neurodevelopmental systems of the mind (attention, memory, language, spatial ordering, sequential ordering, motor, higher thinking, social thinking) in which specific breakdowns in learning manifest themselves in observable behavior. Rather than labeling a student, he suggests that we label the behavior, address the weaknesses, and, in particular, help students build on their strengths.

Levine believes that teachers should analyze the tasks they give to students in order to identify the specific neurodevelopmental functions required of each task. This process of task analysis helps teachers to diagnose the activity instead of the student. Once the problem the student is having with the task has been identified, Levine suggests explaining the problem to the student and then providing him or her with strategies for handling it. Levine's research has shown that students achieve success when they are allowed to learn through their individual strengths, with accommodations and interventions as a secondary focus. Forcing children to do things that their minds aren't wired for can short-circuit their success. We have seen the results of such efforts in our classrooms.

It's taken for granted in adult society that we cannot all be "generalists" skilled in every area of learning and mastery. Nevertheless, we apply tremendous pressure to our children to be good at **everything.** They are expected to shine in math, reading, writing, speaking, spelling, memorization, comprehension, problem solving. . . and none of us adults can do all this.

MEL LEVINE

Below is a list of questions to ask yourself as you analyze your learning tasks to determine which of the eight neurodevelopmental systems are involved and how you can plan for student success.

Things to Consider: Neurodevelopment and Learning

Have I

- ❍ analyzed the task to determine all of the steps and processes it requires students to use?
- ❍ considered whether this task involves attention, memory, language, spatial ordering, sequential ordering, motor skills, higher-order thinking, social skills, or a combination of these?
- ❍ reflected upon what might cause certain students to have difficulty with a particular task?
- ❍ thought of strategies to help those students who need additional assistance and support?
- ❍ considered allowing my students to work on this task using a preferred mode of learning or strength, such as writing about it, talking about it, or drawing an image to make sense of the concept?

online connection

To read articles by Sylwester and others about neuroscience, brain research, and the implications for education, visit the *"News From the Neurosciences"* page of the following Web site:

http://www.newhorizons.org/neuro/front_neuro.html

To learn more about Dr. Mel Levine's approach to understanding and managing differences in learning, visit the following Web site:

http://www.allkindsofminds.org

■ GENDER-BASED PREFERENCES

In addition to learning-style preferences, intelligence preferences, and brain-based differences that exist in the classroom, we also witness gender-based learning preferences on a regular basis. Mark can't sit as still as Shelley, so he rocks in his chair until he periodically falls over. Shelley is a great listener and more comfortable than Mark with a complex flow of conversation. Janine finds math easier to understand when her teacher provides manipulatives for her to use. Damien can calculate numbers more quickly and follow the abstract math lesson taught on the blackboard more easily than Janine.

To understand the *reasons* for the differences in male and female behavior in school, we can turn to the evolutionary biologists. They explain that the brain accommodated to the roles that females and males played for millions of years. Males were responsible for hunting (a spatial occupation) and protection and war (aggressive occupations). Females were responsible for gathering roots and vegetation and most child care (sensory and verbal occupations). Females had to utilize their verbal skills more effectively than males; males had to have finely tuned spatial skills and be more physically aggressive (Gurian, 2001).

In our classrooms today, we often see girls who have better verbal abilities than their male peers and who rely heavily on verbal communication. Frequently, we see boys with better spatial abilities such as measuring, mechanical design, and geography and map reading. Chemicals in the brain tend to make boys more impulsive, as well as fidgety. Girls generally tend not to need movement as much as boys while learning (Gurian, 2001).

To further understand these differences we must look at our social and cultural environments over the past few decades. Until recently, girls were not encouraged to take high-level math and science courses. Therefore, they had little opportunity to excel in those areas. Boys have been encouraged to play sports and with toys like Legos, and this exposure and practice has increased their spatial abilities. The fact that girls tended to have stronger verbal abilities while boys tended to have stronger spatial abilities was generally accepted. Recently, however, educational opportunities have increased for women. Evolutionary neurobiologist Richard C. Francis reports that "the sex differences on standardized math tests has diminished over the past 40 years" (2003). It seems that opportunity and experience can influence success with either gender.

If we are to achieve a richer culture, rich in contrasting values, we must recognize the whole gamut of human potentialities and so weave a less arbitrary social fabric, one in which each diverse human gift will find a future place.

MARGARET MEAD

RELATED LITERATURE

To learn more about gender-based differences, see Michael Gurian's *Boys and Girls Learn Differently: A Guide for Teachers and Parents* (San Francisco: Jossey-Bass, 2001).

Though it's useful to understand differences in brain-based gender preferences, we must be careful not to stereotype students. Great variation exists and there are *many exceptions* to the rules. We should, however, use this new knowledge to add wisdom to our classroom planning and make sure to provide students with choices and flexibility to make their work more productive. The differences between the male and female brain herald a call for differentiation of instruction. The differences point not to a difference in capability, but to the need for different types of learning, different pathways to the same outcome, a differentiated classroom.

Gurian suggests that teachers engage in action-research at the classroom level, and plan same-gender groups for one or more cooperative activities or assignments. He cites examples of teachers from around the country who have used seating charts to separate girls and boys in the middle grades, and who have seen results: With less competition between boys and girls and fewer gender-related psycho-social stressors, gender-grouped classes report greater student achievement and satisfaction in the activity.

I've developed a set of questions that helps me focus on the different physical, social, and academic needs of boys and girls in the classroom. You may want to refer to these questions, listed in the checklist below, to check whether your instructional plans include both learning orientations.

Things to Consider: Gender-based Preferences

Have I

- ❍ planned for boy-only/girl-only groups when useful?
- ❍ offered a balance of sedentary (computer, study, reading) activities with active (group, task-rotation, drama-based) activities in my lessons?
- ❍ provided lots of storytelling and time to explore mythology to help the male brain develop its imaginative and verbal skills through story making?
- ❍ taught higher levels of math not just on the blackboard, which requires abstraction, but also through graphs, charts, written material on paper, and manipulatives, which make abstract ideas more tangible?
- ❍ included a balance of competitive activities and cooperative activities with groups and pairs?

(Based on suggestions from Gurian, 2001)

■ EMOTIONAL INTELLIGENCE

A careful look at our learners reminds us that there are still other ways in which they differ. Each student comes to us with his or her own level of emotional intelligence. Redefining, once again, what it means to be smart, Daniel Goleman, author of the pioneering book on this topic, focuses on a key set of characteristics, including the ability to motivate ourselves and persist in the face of frustrations; to control impulse and delay gratification, to regulate our moods and keep distress from swamping our ability to think, and to empathize and hope (1995). Teaching students to handle anger and resolve conflicts positively, feel empathy, control impulses, and work cooperatively with others increases the likelihood of learner success. By addressing the social and emotional needs of students, teachers can provide safe, respectful, inviting, and engaging environments. It is in these classrooms that students' intellectual lives can flourish because their brains can focus on the cognitive task at hand, rather than on some perceived social or emotional threat.

Arthur Costa and Bena Kallick describe a "character-centered" view of intelligence, one that honors temperament and differences. They list and describe 16 habits that help productive human beings work toward thoughtful, intelligent action when faced with uncertain or challenging situations (2000). Figure 1.4 lists these habits.

Figure 1.4

16 HABITS OF MIND

- Persisting
- Listening with understanding and empathy
- Thinking about thinking (metacognition)
- Questioning and posing problems
- Thinking and communicating with clarity and precision
- Creating, imagining, innovating
- Taking responsible risks
- Thinking interdependently
- Managing impulsivity
- Thinking flexibly
- Striving for accuracy
- Applying past knowledge to new situations
- Gathering data through all the senses
- Responding with wonderment and awe
- Finding humor
- Remaining open to continuous learning

(Costa & Kallick, 2000)

Like Goleman, Costa and Kallick point out that the connection between emotions and intelligence plays a strong role in motivating student behavior. How many of us can point to students whom we have taught strategies and skills only to be frustrated when we realize they are not using the techniques we know they have at their fingertips? When we encourage students to use "habits of mind," we promote the likelihood that they will *choose* to use a strategy or skill that they have been taught. Our classrooms become personal learning laboratories where students discover how they can control their own success by employing certain habits. In one school I work with, three grade levels made habits of mind the focus of character education. Encouraging differentiation, I helped those teachers to develop activities that promoted different learning styles, appealed to multiple intelligences, and employed choice and flexible groupings as they explored these habits with their students. Our project is detailed on page 24.

Consider the habits of mind that you and your students exhibit as you interact and work during the day. You may want to choose one of the habits of mind with which students need support and focus on that habit for a month or focus on several habits over the course of a year.

Things to Consider: Habits of Mind

Have I

❍ made addressing the social and emotional needs of my students a top priority?

❍ identified specific "habits" to work on with my class or particular students?

❍ helped students to set goals in developing these habits?

❍ provided opportunities for students to write, talk, and draw about people in literature, history, science, and their own lives who exhibit these traits?

❍ recognized and honored students who exhibit these traits by creating a "Good Character Club" or a "Healthy Habits of Mind" bulletin board display (photo and description of the habit in action) and encouraged students to recommend their peers for recognition?

A SCHOOL EMBRACES "HABITS OF MIND"

When I helped teachers in Kings Park, New York, implement a "habits of mind" program in their classrooms, we decided to involve teachers, counselors, and administrators in a conversation around developing the new habits. Together, we prioritized and narrowed the list of 16 habits to make it manageable. We decided to focus on the following five habits for the year: persisting, managing impulsivity, listening with understanding and empathy, striving for accuracy, and applying past knowledge to new situations. We shared the list with students and discussed the importance of developing these habits for success in school and beyond.

Agreeing to focus on one habit each month, teachers and counselors provided multiple opportunities for students to talk about, describe, and practice each habit. Here are some of the activities they developed:

- *Classroom discussions:* Using synonyms and descriptions of the "habit in action," students focus on whether characters in literature and movies and people in science, history, and their lives use the habits of mind to succeed. Students are invited to bring in examples of the habit in action from newspaper stories, biographies they've read, or their own journal entries.
- *Bulletin boards:* Students display examples from the lives of remarkable and virtuous people. They may write biographical sketches or create a graphic organizer that highlights the habits of mind that led to the success of their subject.
- *Role play:* Students write skits and role-play the habits of mind in action.
- *Circle-group work:* Students work in a large circle group. The teacher gives them a task, such as orally participating in a Socratic Seminar (see Chapter 6), in order to practice three habits of mind: listening with understanding and empathy, communicating with clarity and precision, and thinking flexibly by looking at alternate points of view.
- *Small-group work:* Students work in small, cooperative groups to complete research or other learning activities with a focus on engaging a particular habit of mind.
- *Character Club:* Students meet in an after-recess club, where they have an opportunity to share incidents in which they or their peers have chosen to use their new habits. Students may receive good character awards to post on a special bulletin board.

RELATED LITERATURE

To learn more about "habits of mind," read Arthur Costa and Bena Kallick's *Discovering and Exploring Habits of Mind.* (Alexandria, Virginia: ASCD, 2000).

Grouped together, student differences might seem overwhelming. How can one teacher manage the learning and intelligence preferences, the thinking styles, the brain-based and gender-based differences, the learning patterns, and the social and emotional needs of an entire class of students?

Most teachers instinctively know there are differences among their students, and they intuitively apply different approaches at a moment's notice. In a differentiated classroom, however, teachers are engaged in the thoughtful and purposeful planning for the range of learners in their classes. Recognizing that they can't fully meet everyone's needs each day, they plan to provide different environments, different learning activities, and different assessments throughout the course of the school year.

Understanding the principles of diversity that we have discussed so far can better prepare you to help students succeed. The rest of this book provides you with a range of concrete strategies for teaching with differentiation in mind. Begin the process of increasing differentiation in your classroom by considering the ways you may already structure your teaching and classroom environment to accommodate student diversity. Use the checklist below to discover areas in which you would like to grow.

Things to Consider

How can I honor the diversity in my classroom? Do I

❍ **frequently assess** the strengths, talents, and interests of my learners through reflective journals, QuickWrites (see Chapter 2), and interest surveys to find out what really motivates them?

❍ **vary my classroom environment** enough so there is a balance of structure and freedom, busyness and quiet, group work and independence?

❍ **rotate the teaching of content** through different learning styles so my students can learn in their preferred style, as well as enlarge their repertoire of skills in their less-preferred styles?

- ❍ **provide enough multiple intelligence–based "choice" opportunities** so my students can choose to learn and show-what-they-know in the ways they prefer?
- ❍ **recognize gender-based differences** in my students and plan a variety of learning opportunities and environments to accommodate those differences?
- ❍ **build the culture of my classroom to reflect a character-centered view of intelligence** in which students are encouraged to persist, resolve conflicts positively, and choose thoughtful, intelligent actions when faced with new situations?
- ❍ **stretch beyond my own teaching style comfort zone** and teach beyond the way I remember being taught?

CHAPTER 2

Differentiating Instruction During the Three Phases of Learning

PRINCIPLES OF EFFECTIVE INSTRUCTION EXPLORED IN THIS CHAPTER:

Multiple pathways to learning

•

Ongoing and frequent assessments

•

Respect for all types of learners

•

The use of brain research

•

Learning styles/Multiple modalities

•

Multiple Intelligences

•

Self-directed learning

As teachers we are sometimes so eager to begin a new unit of study that we dive into the topic without keeping in mind how the brain responds before, during, or after a learning experience. We might ask students, for example, to read ahead for a few pages in the new textbook chapter without remembering that activating prior knowledge *first* is critical to setting a purpose for reading and increasing comprehension. We might feel pressed for time during the unit, and in an effort to cover as much material as we can, we might skip providing time for students to find relevance and construct meaning through elaborative rehearsal with learning partners or cooperative groups, or checking for understanding. Or, when we have covered a topic, we might feel the need to move rapidly on to the next topic in an effort to complete the curriculum. What is lost in this headlong rush is a great deal of understanding, relevancy, and retention.

This chapter presents the research that supports certain types of activities at three different points in the learning process. It also provides examples of specific strategies that you can use to maximize learning at each stage along the way.

KEY IDEA

Student achievement can be enhanced by strategically planning a unit that employs specific strategies before, during, and after the unit.

(MARZANO ET. AL, 2001).

Show Me the Research!

One of the most important things I've learned over the years as a teacher and curriculum designer is the need to plan lessons strategically, using specific methods to elicit critical thinking during three phases of learning: *before, during,* and *after* the learning. Brain-based learning is organized around the principles of how our brain learns best. The more teachers know about how the brain learns and the more research-based instructional strategies we employ, the greater the likelihood that successful learning will occur (Sousa, 2001).

Many researchers have proposed a three-phase learning model. Buehl, Costa, and Garmston identified three phases of cognitive processing. They describe a *preactive phase,* in which the learner is prepared to focus on what is to come, an *interactive phase,* in which the learner selects and organizes the information, and a *reflective phase,* in which the learner integrates and consolidates what has been learned, by applying the knowledge in new situations (Buehl, 1995; Costa and Garmston, 1994, as cited in Billmeyer, 1996).

The PAR teaching model (Preparation, Assistance, and Reflection) described by Richardson and Morgan also shares the before, during, and after framework. Instruction during the *preparation phase* is designed to arouse students' curiosity and their need to know more about the topic. During the *assistance phase,* instruction guides students to make connections and helps them to monitor their understanding. Finally, during the *reflection phase,* opportunities are provided for students to think, talk, and write about the key ideas they've learned, applying and extending new knowledge (Richardson and Morgan, as cited in Billmeyer, 1996).

Additionally, a three-step learning cycle model put forth by Atkin and Karplus (cited by Brooks & Brooks, 1999) describes a first step of *discovery* (working on open-ended exploration with purposefully selected materials), a second step of *concept introduction* (presentation of unfamiliar concepts), and a third step of *concept application* (working on new problems with a new perspective). This constructivist approach to learning places discovery *before* introduction and application. The traditional model of teaching often places discovery at the end of the cycle.

There is a great deal of research to support the three-phase learning model. The more you plan with this model in mind, the more students you will engage in the learning process, and the more effective your lessons will be.

RELATED LITERATURE

To learn more about constructivism, read Jacqueline G. Brooks and Martin G. Brooks's *In search of understanding: The case for constructivist classrooms.* (Alexandria, VA: ASCD, 1999).

Putting Research Into Practice

What can we learn from research on the three phases of learning to make our lessons more effective? By keeping in mind what the brain does during each phase, we can maximize the learning that takes place. By planning multiple activities for each phase and addressing the varied interests, skills, and talents of students, we can apply the principles of differentiation throughout the unit and address the needs of our diverse learners. Here are five guiding points for classroom practice:

- **Pay attention to the critical pre-learning phase.**
- **Provide frequent opportunities throughout a lesson or unit of study for students to make sense of learning.**
- **Allow adequate time for students to process their learning.**
- **Provide closure during the learning process.**
- **Plan time in each lesson for students to reflect upon their learning.**

During the critical, pre-learning phase, schemata (background knowledge structures) are activated, enabling students to use past experiences to interact with new information. A first-step, "discovery" opportunity to interact with purposefully selected materials is the best way for students to construct meaning as they use their prior knowledge. If in our assessment students have no prior experience to which they can easily relate, then we must create a learning experience or provide a model for students to interact with, personalize, and store. In this way, the new, unfamiliar concept can be linked to something they already know. For example, if students have never traveled outside their own community and they are going to be learning about another country or region of the world, it would be helpful to read students a story about that country's cultural heritage or to show them a vivid poster or educational video depicting that country. The story or visual would help them place the learning in context and help them develop a schema for future information to attach itself to.

Provide time and plenty of opportunities for students to participate in **pre-learning** activities. This phase is critical in preparing the learner for all that will follow.

Telling students what they need to know and be able to do by the end of a learning experience will help them attend to what is important and reduce their focus on less important details. This is especially helpful for struggling learners (Wolfe, 2001) who have difficulty with focusing and picking out main ideas. Front-loading information through a variety of strategies (like presenting an advance organizer, introductory summary, or list of helpful terms) is a good way to establish a purpose for learning (Buehl, 1995).

When you provide frequent opportunities throughout a lesson or unit of study for students to make sense of the learning, the learning "sticks." Students require several exposures to content, with different types of expe-

KEY IDEA

During learning allow adequate "wait time" for students to think, process, and note relationships among ideas and concepts.

riences each time, to integrate it into their existing knowledge. For example, Neuthall's research on different types of instruction (1999) shows that students benefit from a variety of instructional types including *dramatic instruction* (role-playing, simulation, storytelling), *verbal instruction* (having students discuss or read about a topic), and *visual instruction* (using forms of graphic representation), with dramatic instruction producing the most learning. Having students listen to or create metaphors and "stories" about the learning enhances their ability to absorb information and provides a needed context for retention. By providing students with multiple exposures to the content over the course of a unit, we create a "spiral" learning model through which we can offer different types of instruction and learning experiences that help meet the needs of diverse learners—and deepen their understanding.

Since the best learning takes place when students make their own connections to the material we teach, we must allow "wait time" (Rowe, 1972) during lessons so that students can think, process, and note relationships among ideas and concepts. Research conducted by J. A. Hobson suggests a "pulse" style of learning is best for the brain (1989). Due to normal fluctuations in brain chemistry, learning attentiveness varies and there is a predictable attention cycle. Eric Jensen notes additional research that suggests taking the age of the student and adding two minutes to determine the amount of time the student can focus on an activity like a lecture (1996). A brief break of about two to five minutes should follow. The break should consist of a "diffusion" activity, a total break from the content, or an alternative form of learning the content.

In addition to allowing wait time, we can facilitate students' ability to process and retain information by providing closure during the learning process. David Sousa describes closure as the process in which the student summarizes for him- or herself what has been learned and attaches sense and meaning to the new learning (2001). He points out that closure increases the likelihood that students retain information in long-term storage and reminds us that closure should take place not only at the end of a lesson or unit, but before a teacher moves from one idea or concept to another *during* a lesson or unit.

KEY IDEA

Post-learning activities should include opportunities for students to form opinions, judge importance, note relationships, take a position, and use the information in new ways.

Finally, students need an opportunity to personalize their learning by reorganizing the information and applying the new knowledge to new situations. Post-learning activities should include opportunities for forming opinions, determining importance, noting relationships, taking a position and providing evidence for that position, creating metaphors and analogies, comparing and contrasting concepts, participating in simulations, and using the new knowledge in different linguistic and nonlinguistic ways. By providing these reflective and summative closure opportunities, we help students to enhance the transfer of information into long-term memory.

Figure 2.1

Three Stages of Learning

Pre-Learning Stage (preactive)
Instruction arouses curiosity, activates and assesses prior knowledge, prepares and focuses students, and provides a first step of "discovery."

During-Learning Stage (interactive)
Teaching guides students to select information, make connections, note relationships, and seek meaning.

Post-Learning Stage (reflective)
Students synthesize what has been learned, reorganize the information, and apply it in new ways.

Strategies

There are dozens of pre-learning, during-learning, and post-learning strategies to choose from when differentiating your instruction to meet the needs of diverse learners. On the lists that follow (pages 33–35), you'll find multiple intelligence–based activities suggested at each stage of learning. Rather than prescribe a set of instructional strategies to use with your class, I have offered a plethora of ideas to allow for your own creativity, teaching style, and the motivation of your very diverse learners. Keep in mind, however, that you will need to stretch beyond your own comfort zone if you are truly going to meet the needs of individual students. Providing an activity that you normally wouldn't think of using might be just the ticket to arousing the interest of that quiet, unmotivated student in the back of your classroom.

As you keep in mind the importance of thoughtfully planning for pre-, during-, and post-learning activities, use the Unit Planner on page 36 to help you vary your lessons and maximize learner success. It provides you with a visual tool for assessing your own instruction and determining whether you are, in fact, addressing the needs of a wide range of learners. Each time you begin a new unit, use the planner to help you choose a variety of multiple intelligence–based strategies for each stage of learning. (See Figure 2.2, which shows a teacher's plan for a unit on the Great Depression.) The planner reminds you to appeal to the talents, interests, and strengths of different kinds of learners and different kinds of minds. (See Chapter 5 for more background on using multiple intelligences theory to inform differentiated instruction.)

Figure 2.2

UNIT
PRE-, DURING-, AND POST-LEARNING ACTIVITIES
PLANNER

Topic/Unit: The Great Depression

Essential Ideas/Key Concepts/Focus Questions:

- Causes
- Hoover's Response
- Impact: Life in cities, culture (changes in society)
- FDR & The New Deal

Key to Multiple Intelligences:

V	Verbal-linguistic	**M**	Musical
L	Logical-mathematical	**I**	Interpersonal
S	Spatial	**A**	Intrapersonal
B	Bodily-kinesthetic	**N**	Naturalist

Pre-Learning Activities: (Activities to hook and focus the learner)

- ❒ B — Present an Artifact Box containing items related to the depression
- ❒ V & L — Present a Concept Map - A graphic organizer of key terms (Ask "what can you tell me about this topic?")
- ❒ S — Show posters & pictures from the time period. - Dust bowl, food lines, California migrant worker

During-Learning Activities: (Activities to help the learner select, organize, and make sense of the information)

- ❒ A — Imagine! Read a student's description of a child living in the dust bowl.
- ❒ V — Stop & Process Activities: QuickWrite / Jot-Pair-Share
- ❒ V-L-A — Note-taking strategies: Interactive Bookmark, Dialectical Journals
- ❒ ___

Post-Learning Activities: (Activities to help the learner reflect and use the information in new ways)

- all students ❒ A — My Opinions Log
- choice:
  - ❒ V-S — Write & illustrate a book to teach a younger child about the depression
  - ❒ I — With a study group, create a graphic organizer.
  - ❒ B-S — Create a Web Page - include images, quotes, sites, Key concepts

A Unit Planner incorporates multiple intelligence–based strategies for each stage of learning.

Activities for the **Pre-Learning** Phase

The following activities and hooks help students prepare, focus, and establish a purpose for learning.

Key to Multiple Intelligences:

A Intrapersonal	**B** Bodily-kinesthetic	**I** Interpersonal
L Logical-mathematical	**M** Musical	**N** Naturalist
S Spatial	**V** Verbal-linguistic	

B V I — **Present a dramatization or read a story** about the new content to provide context. (For example, have a colleague unexpectedly come into your classroom and read a list of unreasonable school rules and additional lunch taxes that have suddenly been put into place. After the reader warns students to comply or face no lunch, detention, or worse and abruptly leaves, have students discuss their reactions. This can lead into a lesson about dictators, tyranny, revolution, etc.)

B N — **Let students engage in an open-ended exploration with selected materials to discover concepts and relationships.** Encourage discovery through observation (How do the ants survive in this colony?) and manipulation (What forces are involved as my toy car goes down a ramp?).

N — **Show the phenomenon!** Ask students to describe what is happening as you perform a science demonstration.

S M N — **Show a video clip or PowerPoint presentation, play an audiotape or piece of music, present posters or models.** Have students record observations, predictions, or inferences. Ask them to describe, note relationships, or compare and contrast.

B A N — **Present an Artifact Box** (social studies/science/math/foreign language) or **Treasure Chest** (English). Ask students to rearrange the artifacts and tell you about the topic, time period, culture, region, event, story, or character from the items, photos, pictures, quotes, etc., in front of them. (See pages 37–39 for teaching ideas and an example of an Artifact Box.)

V L — **Present a Concept Map (a web of key terms) about the new topic/reading.** Ask students what they can tell you about the topic or upcoming reading and set it in a visual format for reference.

V I — **Have students brainstorm what they already know** using a K-W-L Chart, a WordSplash!, or a class web.

V L — **Model a Text Walk.** Teach students how to read a textbook by modeling how to skim and thinking aloud for them. Point out nonfiction text elements, such as chapter subheadings, charts, graphs, maps, pictures with captions, timelines, summaries, and lists of terms.

V L B — **Have students engage in a Text Scavenger Hunt.** After modeling a Text Walk for several chapters, provide sticky notes and have students tab answers to five questions you pose about the upcoming reading. Without reading the text, have students skim and search for the answers in the subheadings, charts, graphs, maps, pictures with captions, timelines, summaries, lists of terms, etc.

V L B **Have students engage in a Chapter Prediction.** After having students practice for several chapters how to skim a textbook (see Text Scavenger Hunt above), ask students to predict what a new chapter will be about without reading it. Provide sticky notes for students to tab and record five important ideas they believe will be presented in the upcoming chapter.

Activities for the **During-Learning** Phase

The following activities help students select and organize information. They engage the learner in making sense and meaning (seeking understanding and relevance) throughout the learning.

S **Picture This!** Have students close their eyes and picture in their minds any scene, event, object, situation, or scientific principle that you describe or read to them. The image they envision will help the brain retain the information. After they open their eyes, let them write or draw a summary of what they've heard.

A **Imagine!** Ask students to imagine they are part of an event, scene, or situation that you are studying. Have them write point-of-view journal entries. By personalizing the information, it becomes more relevant to the learner and, therefore, more likely to be remembered.

V I **Use Stop-and-Process activities many times throughout your lessons to provide wait time for student thinking and to check for understanding. (See descriptions in this chapter for elaboration about Stop-and-Process activities.)**

- **Stop and Jot:** a two- to five-minute check for understanding in which the student records his or her perception of key ideas and concepts or answers a question in a boldly colored "stop box"
- **Jot-Pair-Share:** an opportunity for each student to record her *own* thoughts *before* moving into pairs to discuss ideas with others
- **QuickWrite** or **Non-Stop!:** a *timed* piece of writing (90 seconds to two minutes) on a specific topic. It can be a "freewrite" ("Write everything you know about fractions"), a response to a given question or statement ("Which side do you believe had the greatest advantages during the Civil War, the North or the South?"), or a summary about a topic using specific terms ("Using the following terms, describe what impact geography had on the development of Greek civilization").

V **Use metaphors for key concepts.** Metaphors promote the transfer of information by helping to convey meaning. ("Imperialism is like a bully on the playground.")

I **Provide frequent opportunities for students to engage in Partner Talks.** Partner Talks encourage students to explain or describe to a peer in their own words what they are learning. This promotes students' abilities to process, store, and use information. (See Chapter 6 for further discussion about learning in partnerships.)

A V S **Use Interactive Bookmarks with textbooks and/or novels.** Interactive Bookmarks allow students to "chunk" their reading and respond in ways that personally engage them. (See pages 41 and 42 for teaching ideas and an example of Interactive Bookmarks.)

V L A **Provide students with a variety of note-taking strategies including Dialectical Journals and Noting What I've Learned to help them organize their thoughts.** (See Chapter 3 for teaching ideas and examples of Choice Note-Taking.)

B **Provide opportunities for students to engage in kinesthetic activities.** Using instructional materials with which students can physically interact, such as rulers, lab equipment, tiles, blocks, sentence strips, flashcards, props, pictures, news articles, rocks, and collections of things, allow students to build, sort, group, organize, hypothesize, and otherwise make sense of the world around them.

V L B **Have students Post-a-Point!** Using sticky notes, students identify key elements in their reading. They use the notes for writing and communicating ideas based in text. (See pages 39 and 40 for teaching ideas and an example for Language Arts.)

Activities for the **Post-Learning** Phase

The following activities help students reflect upon new knowledge and make personal links and connections in order to facilitate transfer into long-term memory.

V S L **Have students complete a Sum-It-Up!** to show what they've learned at the end of a lesson or unit. (See pages 45 and 46 for teaching ideas and a Sum-It-Up! example.)

V A **Assign an ongoing My Opinions Journal:** At the end of each unit, have students generate at least three opinions about a topic or theme they've studied. Note the key concepts learned. Ask them to determine the importance of each, note relationships, compare and contrast new information with other things they've learned, support their opinions with evidence (facts, examples, quotes, etc.). Also, have them predict how the information learned in this unit can be used in the future. (See Chapter 6 for more teaching ideas.)

L S I **Have students gather data or research something new** about the topic and present the new information in a chart or graph to the class. Encourage them to draw at least two conclusions from their own research.

I L **Organize study groups and have the groups create a graphic organizer** that organizes ideas from this unit.

V B M **Make creative presentations an option:** Let students choose whether they want to
- write and/or act out a story that dramatizes the information in the unit or
- write and/or present a song or poem that summarizes the information in this unit.

V S **Have students write and illustrate a book to teach a younger child** about the key concepts of this unit.

S **Make a class Unit Collage** (see Chapter 5 for teaching ideas) to synthesize and summarize the unit.

I **Create a Newscast** and let students choose different roles to play (eyewitness reporter, anchor, etc.) to teach about multiple perspectives of important events, key figures and their contributions, and other important ideas from this unit.

B L **Show students how to make their own Artifact Box** (see Pre-Learning Activities) that includes items such as photos, quotes, pictures, and symbols that represent the main concepts and themes studied. Include a written description of each item's significance.

B S **Let students create a Web page** that brings together information, images, quotes, and Web sites on this topic.

UNIT

PRE-, DURING-, AND POST-LEARNING ACTIVITIES

PLANNER

Topic/Unit: ______________________________

Essential Ideas/Key Concepts/Focus Questions:

- ______________________________
- ______________________________
- ______________________________
- ______________________________

Key to Multiple Intelligences:				
	V	Verbal-linguistic	**M**	Musical
	L	Logical-mathematical	**I**	Interpersonal
	S	Spatial	**A**	Intrapersonal
	B	Bodily-kinesthetic	**N**	Naturalist

Pre-Learning Activities: (Activities to hook and focus the learner)

❒ ________ ______________________________

❒ ________ ______________________________

❒ ________ ______________________________

During-Learning Activities: (Activities to help the learner select, organize, and make sense of the information)

❒ ________ ______________________________

❒ ________ ______________________________

❒ ________ ______________________________

❒ ________ ______________________________

Post-Learning Activities: (Activities to help the learner reflect and use the information in new ways)

❒ ________ ______________________________

❒ ________ ______________________________

❒ ________ ______________________________

❒ ________ ______________________________

Strategies

I've selected several activities from each learning phase and described in detail how you can use them to engage different types of learners. The Artifact Box and Post-a-Point! activities are designed to appeal to kinesthetic students who like to use their hands when learning. The Interactive Bookmark and Stop-and-Process activities (including Stop and Jot, Jot-Pair-Share, QuickWrite, Sum-It-Up!, and Exit Cards) may appeal to students who need time to process information in chunks before moving on to something new. The opportunity to write down or draw about what they have been listening to helps visual learners to be more successful in their typically auditory classrooms.

Artifact Box **(Pre-Learning)**

The kinesthetic learner in your classroom will love the opportunity to create an **Artifact Box**. Placed in a shoebox or large plastic container, an Artifact Box (or Treasure Chest) is a collection of items—such as symbols, photos, charts, graphs, quotes, audiotapes, drawings, and sketches—that represent key ideas about a topic. It can be presented by the teacher to *introduce* a unit, or gathered by students to show-what-they-know *at the end* of a unit. Alternatively, students can gather symbolic representations of each subtopic learned *throughout* the unit of study, creating an *ongoing* class Artifact Box.

To present this as a pre-learning activity, ask students to examine, group, and rearrange the collection of items that you have provided in order to make sense of what the collection represents. For example, having gathered a collection of items that reflect immigration during the eighteenth and nineteenth centuries—a photo of a starving family on a farm in Ireland, a poster of a pogrom (organized massacre) in Russia, a model of the Statue of Liberty, a picture of a crowded tenement apartment in New York City, a potato, a gold coin, a photo of sick children dying from typhoid and cholera in a slum in Chicago, and photos of garment workers in New York City, Chinese immigrants working on the railroads, and coal miners in the Midwest—you could ask students to examine the items to discover why millions of people came to America and what life was like when they first arrived. By observing, manipulating, and grouping a collection of items, students can discover much about a topic. Through sensory exploration they become engaged, begin to make predictions, and develop schema to enhance further learning.

Once you have modeled what can go into an Artifact Box, you and your students can gather one together over the course of a new unit. For example, as you read a novel, you and your students can place items in a box that represent the main characters (a sketch of the character or an important quote copied onto an index card), the setting (a map or sketch of a location), the conflict (a symbolic drawing), and the themes (a heart-

TEACHER REFLECTION

My students are eager to think of items to place in our Artifact Boxes. They really get creative as they search for symbols on the Internet or draw pictures to be included. Some students like to write diary entries and quotes for the characters, some draw the settings and pivotal scenes, some audiotape important passages or find music on the Internet to reflect our topic or theme. Almost every student gets eagerly involved in some way.

—MIDDLE-SCHOOL TEACHER

shaped box to represent love or a water canteen to represent survival). Students can draw the items or bring them in from home throughout the reading of the novel. This during-learning activity will give students an opportunity to stop and process concepts in symbolic, more abstract ways, increasing the likelihood of retention. By the end of the reading, the box of items can be displayed to help students vividly see and conceptualize important ideas and lessons learned from the reading.

As an end-of-unit project, individual students or small groups of students can gather their own collection of items to demonstrate their analysis of the topic. For example, after studying the different biomes in the world, groups can be organized to gather items representing the landforms, the plant and animal life, the natural resources, the climate, and the occupations associated with each biome. After each group presents its collection to the class, other students can be asked to choose the five most important or representative artifacts from the group's display to include in a biome museum exhibit and to write a brief description about the significance of each item. This will help students to pick out key ideas and make connections, noting relationships among climate, natural resources, and occupations, for example.

Be sure to save your Artifact Boxes so that next year you can use them as advance organizers (introductions to a unit as part of the pre-learning stage). You may also want to be able to mix the items from two or more different Artifact Boxes and have students group and classify the items for comparison and contrast. Since the brain is a category seeker, this activity will help students remember what they've learned. It will help them compare information and note patterns and then encode the information more easily for future retrieval.

An Artifact Box or Treasure Chest can be gathered for any content area. See Figures 2.3 and 2.4 for examples of Artifact Boxes for Math and Social Studies.

Figure 2.3

A Fractions Artifact Box (Math)

This artifact box might include:

- ✔ pictures drawn to name a part of one thing *(two slices of pizza, eight slices of pizza in all; 2/8)*
- ✔ pictures from a magazine labeled to name part of a collection of things *(four children in the picture, eight people in total in the picture; 4/8)*
- ✔ measuring cups
- ✔ recipe cards
- ✔ measuring spoons
- ✔ a ruler
- ✔ linking cubes
- ✔ a calculator
- ✔ drawings of equivalent fractions
- ✔ a number line ordering the numbers from least to greatest

Figure 2.4

A Civil War Artifact Box (Social Studies)

This artifact box might include:

- ✔ A book cover from *Uncle Tom's Cabin*
- ✔ Color printouts of flags of the Union and of the Confederacy
- ✔ An 1850s map showing free states and slave states
- ✔ A sketch of the bombardment of Fort Sumter
- ✔ A timeline of the Civil War
- ✔ A poster to warn slaves about kidnappers and slave catchers
- ✔ An audiotape of the Lincoln–Douglas Debates reenacted
- ✔ A photo of Harriet Tubman and Sojourner Truth
- ✔ A set of headlines—one from a Southern paper, one from a Northern paper—about two important Civil War incidents
- ✔ A toy suitcase covered in "carpet" (representing the "carpetbaggers")

Post-a-Point! **(During-Learning)**

The biggest problem students have with reading their textbooks is staying awake. There is too much information for them to process in one continuous reading.

Post-a-Point! is a kinesthetic strategy that "chunks" the reading, engaging readers to interact with text and helping them to focus on important elements.

Students strategically place sticky notes on the pages they are reading and record abbreviations for key concepts (and make other notes or drawings) to help make the text memorable. With a partner, they discuss what they've found, and through this conversation and others with the teacher and the whole class, they come to know and understand the ideas found in the text. This kinesthetic and visual strategy helps students become more active readers and ultimately improves their comprehension. The partner and group discussions help them to make sense of the information.

Used in a social studies class, this strategy helps students to focus on the concepts and themes that serve as content organizers for the vast amount of information to be learned. Used in an English class with literature, this strategy allows students to note story elements and figurative language. By posting these elements, students can later find important information or evidence from text when speaking or writing in response to the literature. They can quickly find textual material to support their ideas, make connections, or note relationships. The identification of key concepts helps students who need more time sorting learning into important and nonimportant categories focus on what really matters. By focusing on the big ideas and paying less attention to irrelevant details, these students can now think more critically and move up Bloom's Taxonomy with greater success. (See Chapter 4 for more on Bloom's Taxonomy and effective instruction.)

To introduce this strategy to students, brainstorm with your class a list of abbreviations for key concepts within the subject area in focus (see Figure 2.5). The abbreviations make note-taking on the sticky notes quick, easy, and identifiable. Choosing just a few of these abbreviations, model through shared reading how you would identify key concepts and strategically place sticky notes in the text. Show students how you might add brief notes or draw a symbol to help you remember what you are reading.

Next, have partners read silently, post their notes on the passage individually, and then come together to share what they have learned. Through discussion and meeting with different partners, students will learn more about how best to use the strategy. Finally, they will be ready to use it on their own during independent reading assignments. Slowly, over time, add to the list of abbreviations to be used for independent reading. Have students partner the day after homework to discuss what they learned.

Figure 2.5

Post-a-Point! (Language Arts)

The following terms are standards-based language that students must understand to master concepts in English. When responding to literature in class or on state or federal assessments, students must be able to locate evidence from text to support their ideas. In this kinesthetic activity, students practice taking note of important literary elements as they read.

Encourage students to interact with text as they read by having them place sticky notes on pages where they find examples of the following terms. Show them how to record on the sticky notes brief notes and/or symbols that will help them make an association that they'll remember.

Literary terms and abbreviations or symbols:

- Setting (time or place) (clock symbol)
- Character attributes (important traits, key quotes and actions, and what others say about the character) (C)
- Plot (events in the story) PL
- Conflict (internal or external conflicts; man vs. himself, man vs. man, man vs. society, man vs. nature) →←
- Motive (the impulse, reason, or desire that leads to action) M ?
- Theme (the central message) (T)
- Symbolism (emotions expressed through symbols) ♡
- Figurative Language/Figures of Speech (metaphor, simile, irony, imagery, etc.) (Fig.)
- Connections (personal connections, connections between this text and another, connections between this text and something in the real world) (interlocking circles)

The Interactive Bookmark **(During-Learning)**

The **Interactive Bookmark** is a note-taking tool for students to use as they read independently. Designed to help students stop and process at different points throughout their reading, the Interactive Bookmark is an open-ended activity that includes both linguistic and nonlinguistic elements. In fact, the two different templates on reproducible page 42 provide a choice for students to just use words or to include symbols and nonlinguistic elements for note-taking. The bookmark invites readers at different levels of proficiency to choose the way they respond to text. You can expand students' abilities to respond when they use the bookmark by providing mini-lessons on specific strategies that target areas in which students need support, such as identifying cause-and-effect relationships, recognizing text structure, paraphrasing, inferring, and summarizing. The bookmark can be a practice tool students use to become strategic readers.

Students respond in many different ways to literature by writing and/or drawing on their Interactive Bookmarks.

As always, introduce the activity by modeling it. Provide students with copies of the Interactive Bookmark (have these precut or ask students to cut out their own). Read aloud an engaging book and stop at key points in the text (e.g., the middle of a heated dialogue or the end of an extended description). At each stopping point ask students to respond on their bookmarks to what they have read, filling in the boxes on their bookmark and labeling the box with the chapter and page or paragraph number. Share several student responses with the whole class.

When students are ready to use the bookmark independently, assign students a few "stop points" in their reading and give them the choice of only a few options for response at each stop point. Add options as students learn what a quality response looks like in each case. Figure 2.6 lists a variety of ways students can respond to what they are reading.

Figure 2.6

WAYS FOR STUDENTS TO RESPOND TO TEXTS

- Jot down a key idea expressed by the author.
- Paraphrase what you have read.
- Draw a symbol or picture to help you remember an important part.
- Make note of something important (a quotation, a theme).
- Make a connection between this text and your own experiences.
- Make a connection between this text and another.
- Make a connection between this text and something in the real world.
- Write two questions that can be answered by the reading.
- Predict what will happen next.
- Note evidence of text structure.
- Identify a confusing part.
- Pose a question you want answered.
- Give your opinion of what you read.
- Create a metaphor or simile to help you remember an important word or idea (____ *is like* ____).

_______________'s

INTERACTIVE BOOKMARK

BOOK TITLE OR TEXTBOOK PAGES

____

STOP point #1 _______________

____

____

____

STOP point #2 _______________

____

____

____

STOP point #3 _______________

____

____

____

STOP point #4 _______________

____

____

____

Notes: _______________

____

____

_______________'s

INTERACTIVE BOOKMARK

BOOK TITLE OR TEXTBOOK PAGES

____

STOP point #1

____

STOP point #2

____

STOP point #3

____

STOP point #4

____

Notes: _______________

____

____

Stop-and-Process Activities

When I work with teachers to improve student comprehension and retention during learning, I always focus their attention on Stop-and-Process activities. These quick checks for understanding help *all* students make sense of what they are learning, but they are particularly helpful to struggling learners. These students often need more time to process what they hear. They need to see something in writing in order to make the information more memorable. They need a few moments to catch up. Too often, we have quickly moved on.

The Stop-and-Process strategies I recommend are easy to use. Stop and Jots, Jot-Pair-Share, QuickWrites, Sum-It-Up!'s, and Exit Cards give students time to pause, reflect, and write or draw to help make information memorable. The variety of strategies appeals to a range of learners because some activities involve writing, others drawing, and still others involve interacting with peers. Because the strategies are generally open-ended, students can respond to these Stop-and-Process activities at their own level of readiness.

Most of the activities can be used at the beginning of a lesson (as a formative assessment) to help students activate prior knowledge and to help teachers assess what students already know. They can also be used during the middle of a lesson (as a medial assessment) to provide students with adequate opportunity to make sense of information and provide teachers with a tool to check for understanding. Finally, they can be used at the end of a lesson (as a summative assessment) to provide an opportunity for closure and a quick check, once again, for understanding and/or misconceptions. Embedded in daily teaching and learning, these thinking strategies engage our learners in deeper processing and provide us with quick and ongoing assessments of our students, informing our instruction each step of the way (Figure 2.7).

Figure 2.7

WHEN TO USE STOP-AND-PROCESS ACTIVITIES

As a Formative Assessment

- To activate prior knowledge (what background knowledge, structures, or schemata are already in place?)
- To assess prior knowledge (what do they already know?)
- To inform instruction (what can you learn about students and their knowledge to plan lessons thoughtfully and purposefully?)

As a Medial Assessment

- To provide "wait time" for processing
- To provide time for students to create a written summary of an auditory lesson
- To provide closure before moving from one sub-topic or skill to another during a lesson
- To inform instruction

As a Summative Assessment

- To check for understanding and/or misconceptions
- To see student thinking about the key ideas of the lesson or unit
- To provide an opportunity for students to respond to the essential questions of the lesson or unit
- To provide time for students to find personal relevance in the learning, to make connections, and to note relationships

TEACHER REFLECTION

Frequent Stop-and-Jots are the perfect solution to keeping some very distractible students on task!

— FOURTH-GRADE TEACHER

Stop and Jot **(During- & Post-Learning)**

A **Stop and Jot** is a two- to five-minute check for understanding. Students each record their perception of a key idea or concept about a topic or reading in a boldly colored rectangle that they have drawn on their paper or in their notebook. At least once during a lesson, stop and pose an important question for students to respond to in their quickly drawn "stop box." Have volunteers share one or two responses with the whole class, or model your own response on the chalkboard or overhead. These boxes serve to aid students later as a study tool, standing out with their bright colors and highlighting important information from the reading or about the topic.

Jot-Pair-Share **(During- & Post-Learning)**

A **Jot-Pair-Share** is adapted from the Think-Pair-Share activity (Lyman, 1981) in which students are provided time to think and then talk about a topic in pairs before speaking in front of the whole class. I prefer that each student not just think, but record, or jot down, his or her thoughts *before* pairing with a partner. This can significantly change what takes place during the pairing. In the original activity, the partner who is more verbal, more outgoing, and quicker to process information will likely present his or her ideas first. The other partner may shut down, agreeing with the points just made and making no original contribution of his or her own. By having both partners jot first, each one is more likely to have something to share. Through this brief conversation in which students "do the explaining," we address the need for learners to articulate concepts in their own words and to learn from one another, but we also keep them focused by providing a specific task to complete or question to answer.

Whoever explains learns.
DAVID SOUSA

QuickWrite **(During- & Post-Learning)**

A **QuickWrite** is a timed piece of writing on a topic posed by the teacher. Students are given between 90 seconds and two minutes to write freely or respond to a given question or statement ("Tell me how decimals and fractions are related." "How does geography affect the occupations of people in different parts of the world?"). This activity gives students time to process auditory information, and it frees the teacher up to go over to struggling learners who might need additional guidance in thinking about the topic. QuickWrites invite students to use the vocabulary of a discipline to express their knowledge. In fact, you can provide students with important terms and ask them to use several of those terms in their writing. Because the activity is limited to a short amount of time, even reluctant writers are willing to communicate their ideas in this way.

Sum-It-Up! **(Post-Learning)**

I developed **Sum-It-Up!** a number of years ago when I was creating activities for closure and for improving study skills. This quick assessment tool addresses the need for visual learners to record and draw their ideas in order to make sense of them. Although teachers have used them in countless ways since, the original intent was to provide a format for students to record a summary of a particular lesson each day. If you choose to use the reproducible form, make copies of page 46 for each student. On Monday at the end of a lesson, select a topic or question to which students will respond. Have them copy this information in the top left box and set aside five to seven minutes for students to fill in the What I Learned box with a written description or descriptive sketch of the material they've learned. By Friday, each student will have a one-page overview of what they've learned about the topic. More important, students can use the form as a study tool by folding the page to cover up their What I Learned Statement and testing themselves on the material.

Over the course of many workshops, teacher-participants have taught me many ways to refine the use of this tool, including creating three-hole-punched Sum-It-Up! forms on a different color paper for each subject, having students attach three weeks of Sum-It-Up! forms to their unit exam in order to receive bonus points, and placing the lesson objective in the left column and having students respond or reflect upon it in the right column as an immediate and quick assessment during closure. Of all the strategies I have shared with teachers over the years, this has been one of the most widely used by teachers of every grade level.

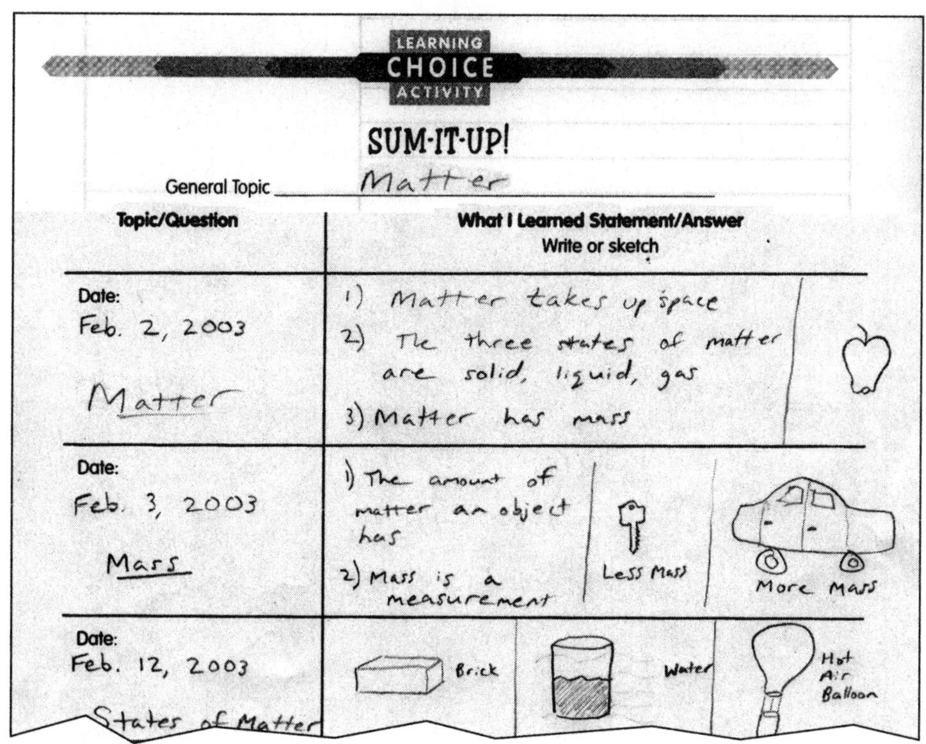

LEARNING CHOICE ACTIVITY

SUM-IT-UP!

General Topic Matter

Topic/Question	What I Learned Statement/Answer Write or sketch
Date: Feb. 2, 2003 Matter	1) Matter takes up space 2) The three states of matter are solid, liquid, gas 3) Matter has mass
Date: Feb. 3, 2003 Mass	1) The amount of matter an object has 2) Mass is a measurement Less Mass / More Mass
Date: Feb. 12, 2003 States of Matter	Brick / Water / Hot Air Balloon

TEACHER REFLECTION

Using Stop-and-Process strategies has made a big difference. Instead of moving like an express train from minute one to minute 42, I now move more like a local train making stops throughout my class session—I find I pick up more passengers along the way!

—CINDY STERN
LONG BEACH SCHOOLS

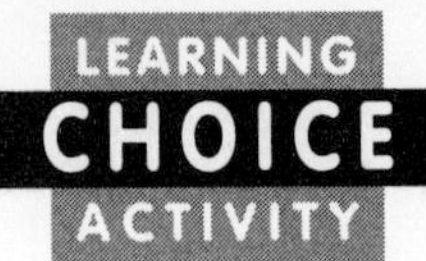

SUM-IT-UP!

General Topic ____

Topic/Question	**What I Learned Statement/Answer** (Write or sketch)
Date:	
Date:	
Date:	
Date:	
Date:	

Exit Card **(During- & Post-Learning)**

An **Exit Card** is a tool that you can use at the end of a lesson to inform your instruction. As students leave the classroom, they hand you an index card with their response to a question you've asked (about the lesson, for example) or with a self-assessment describing how well they applied a new rule or principle, such as solving a problem using a newly learned math formula. Students tend to pay very close attention when teachers make Exit Cards a frequent part of closure.

Using this student-generated data, you can quickly assess your students' knowledge and categorize learners into three groups, those who are uncertain or confused, those who need a little more practice, and those who have mastered the concept. In five minutes, you can determine which students need your special attention before going on. You can provide struggling learners with five to ten minutes of scaffolding the next day during a warm-up time or you can challenge advanced learners through a targeted conversation.

This sorting of students by need might also lead you to a tiered lesson tomorrow. With Exit Card responses, you can easily group students *fairly* and *appropriately* for leveled activities. (See Figure 2.8 for examples of Exit Cards. See Chapter 7 for a discussion of how to use tiered assignments with flexible groupings.)

Figure 2.8

Examples of Exit Cards

Using the map on page 216 and what you know about geography, describe what life must be like in the city of Seattle, Washington. (Social Studies)	You have a shelf that is 4½ feet long. How many ½-foot-long boxes can you store on the shelf? (Math)
Having read and analyzed Langston Hughes's poem *Mother to Son,* in which a mother compares life to a staircase, create your own metaphor for life. (Include at least two comparisons.) (Language Arts)	Using the two food labels provided, decide whether these foods are healthy to eat. Give your opinion and support it with evidence. (Health)

TEACHER REFLECTION

I have used Exit Cards as a quick assessment tool to help me decide whether or not I need to give more time to a particular topic. From the information I gather, I put students into groups for review, practice, or challenge activities. I have used the cards with math and writing concepts, story comprehension, and social studies terms. Because of my regular use of Exit Cards, my students have come to understand that they are accountable for their learning at all times, whether they are engaged in whole-group lessons, small groups, partner work, or individual activities.

—JANE WHEARTY
MINEOLA SCHOOLS

Allison Sept.21,2004
• graphs have axes going vertical, and horizontil
• graphs usually have titles
• the bars on a graph can go vertical or horizontal
• the axes must be detailed
• there must be a zero in the corner of the axes.

Jonathan 9-21-04

Graphs need two lines. One line goes horizontally and one goes virdicly. You need data to make a graph. You need a title. You need tallymarks to make a graph. You should have bars and numbers next to the horizontal line. You could put numbers going next to the virdical line. You don't have to but should make it cobrful.

Students' Exit Card responses to a teacher's prompt: "Tell me everything you've learned about graphs."

By integrating different types of activities at each of the three stages of learning, you increase the likelihood that learning is taking place throughout a lesson. In Chapter 3 you'll learn ways to help students find meaning or personal relevance in the learning process. As David Sousa reminds us, when students find both sense and meaning in what you teach, they will be more likely to remember it.

CHAPTER 3

Providing Choice During Instruction

PRINCIPLES OF EFFECTIVE INSTRUCTION EXPLORED IN THIS CHAPTER:

Multiple pathways to learning

•

Respect for all types of learners

•

Reducing anxiety

•

The use of brain research

•

Multiple intelligences

•

Intrinsic motivation

•

Choice

•

Constructivist practices

•

Self-directed learning

•

A student-centered classroom

I often begin my differentiating instruction workshops by asking teachers to tell me what it's like to manage a multilevel classroom. Inevitably they report frustrations about the difficulties of keeping interest high for advanced students while tending to the needs of struggling learners. The theme I hear most often in these conversations is the lack of motivation on the part of students of all readiness levels.

Many teachers argue that if they had all advanced learners, motivation would not be an issue. If motivation is defined in terms of a student's inclination to complete the task assigned, in a sense, the teachers would be correct. Most advanced learners, those who perform well, will often do what is needed to get their A's and give their teachers exactly what has been asked for, but nothing more.

Other teachers point out that they have many students who can but won't do what is asked of them, choosing instead to just get by in class. Finally, teachers talk about their students who are unable to complete the assigned task because the task requires a particular skill they may not have developed yet.

Certainly, this presents a dilemma for teachers. But it is not insurmountable. One of the easiest ways to change student attitudes toward completing homework, class work, and research, is to provide choices. When choice is given to students about the way they can show-what-they-know, struggling learners find a way to demonstrate their understanding,

If a student has the mindset not to comply, nothing you do can make him. We cannot use external motivation to force, bully, or coerce a student to learn. Internal motivation, however, guides all human behavior. We can create the conditions where students choose to learn.

J.C. ERWIN

average students choose tasks that intrigue them, and more advanced learners take off in ways we could never have imagined. Choice is a key to motivation in your classroom.

Show Me the Research!

Eric Jensen claims there is no such thing as an unmotivated learner (1996). There are, however, times when students experience low motivation in response to a particular learning situation, and these times can be a daily source of frustration for teachers. When they are unmotivated, students usually do little or no work and often act out in class. Motivated students, on the other hand, usually turn in high-quality work, learn well, and behave responsibly (Erwin, 2003).

To understand how we can motivate our students, we must turn to William Glasser's Choice Theory (1998), which explains the benefits of intrinsic motivation over extrinsic motivation. When teachers use *external motivation*, they rely heavily on rewards and punishments, and they assume the full responsibility for motivating their students. External motivation can come in the form of test grades, bonus points, points lost, and pizza parties, all within the teacher's control. When teachers use *internal motivation*, they inspire the natural drives within the learner, thus creating the conditions for their students to be motivated and assume some of the responsibility for that motivation (Erwin, 2003). Internal motivation feeds a student's sense of curiosity, love of fun, and desire for power and freedom. With a little creativity, you can create the kind of environment in which students want to take more responsibility for their learning.

As teachers, from time to time we all wonder, "What am I doing wrong with this class?" Nothing seems to inspire active involvement. Students are fidgety or less engaged than we had hoped. Motivation seems minimal. *We* seem to be doing all of the work.

At these times, we need to take a close look at what we're doing and honestly appraise whether we are creating any of the conditions that Jensen (1996) suggests demotivate learners:

- repetitive, rote learning
- top-down management
- boring, single-media presentations
- reward systems of any kind
- teaching to just one or two of the multiple intelligences

We need to consider the conditions that we can establish in our classrooms to foster intrinsic motivation. The following section outlines some practical ways to apply the research on motivation to classroom settings. Our goal is to engage students in ways that ensure they are both excited about and invested in their work.

Putting Research Into Practice

Glasser's Choice Theory suggests that warm, supportive human relationships are extremely important to student success in school. By showing students that we care enough about them to learn about their interests and to give them choices in their learning, we create the environment where students *want* to behave responsibly and *want* to learn. Glasser points out that in addition to the need for survival, there are four psychological needs that drive all human endeavors: the need to belong, the need for power, the need for freedom, and the need for fun.

In a differentiated classroom we address these needs by creating opportunities for students to express themselves individually or to work with others, by allowing students to choose activities of interest that are playful yet challenging and by empowering students through active learning and decision making. When you allow students the choice of working alone or working with others, you address their need for belonging. When you put students in charge of choosing which activity to complete, you address their need for power and freedom. When you offer students creative ways to show-what-they-know, you address their need for fun. The more we address these needs, the more we foster intrinsic motivation in learners.

TEACHER REFLECTION

I have been amazed by the quality of work handed in when I have allowed my students to show-what-they-know in ways they prefer. Students who rarely speak in class have made oral presentations of more than five minutes. The pride they felt in their work was quite obvious. Because it appealed to the interests of my inclusion students while simultaneously addressing the issue of their readiness, the work they produced was comparable to the strongest of students. I now can't imagine teaching without differentiating my instruction.

—RYAN TORMEY
SEVENTH-GRADE ENGLISH TEACHER

Things to Consider: Intrinsic Motivation

How can I foster intrinsic motivation in learners? Do I

- ❍ teach students to work cooperatively with others?
- ❍ give students a voice in classroom decision making?
- ❍ provide opportunities for students' personal growth?
- ❍ teach to a variety of learning styles?
- ❍ recognize and address different readiness levels?
- ❍ provide students with choices?
- ❍ use a variety of instructional strategies?
- ❍ offer fun activities that inspire creativity and reduce stress?

Finding times for choice opportunities throughout your instructional routine helps you differentiate your content, your learning activities, and your assessments (content, process, and product). By offering different reading selections based on readiness rather than assigning all students the same chapter in a textbook or providing different research topics based on interest, you accommodate students with a choice of content. By presenting different homework options, class activities, or note-taking strategies, you

Information is most likely to get stored if it makes sense and has meaning. Imagine the many hours that go into planning and teaching lessons, and it all comes down to these two questions: "Does this make **sense?**" (does it fit into what the learner knows) and "Does this have **meaning?**" (is it relevant to the learner).

DAVID SOUSA

help students to choose their most comfortable way to process, or make sense of, the information. By suggesting different research methods, resources, presentation strategies, and reporting formats, you allow for diversity in end-of-unit products or assessments.

The goal of these choice opportunities is to engage each learner in relevant activities that are personally meaningful and appropriately challenging. Such opportunities can also foster independence and provide practice for self-directed learning. By creating a more responsive classroom where students are given a voice and provided options that match their needs, talents, and interest, we differentiate our classrooms and show respect for all types of learners. We provide an environment in which our students will find ways to connect to the learning and find a purpose for learning it.

The teacher benefits from choice opportunities, as well. Instead of assessing 30 (or 130!) essay reports on the same topic, he or she now accepts multiple products that allow students to explore, debate, design, and experiment in various ways they've chosen to demonstrate their understanding of a topic.

By providing choice, we do much to create an environment in which students are intrinsically motivated to learn. When we offer choice to students, we are saying "we care about you." When students feel teachers care about them, they come to our classrooms more eagerly; they are more willing to become engaged in our lessons. As Erwin concludes, appealing to students' needs for belonging, power, freedom, and fun will dramatically increase the likelihood that students will behave responsibly and want to learn what we want to teach.

A Dr. Seuss game board is the logical-mathematical option one student chose to show-what-she-knows about the author and his work.

Strategies

Following are some motivating strategies to support you as you find ways to provide students with choices in their learning on a regular basis. Offering Choice Homework on a weekly or biweekly schedule, presenting multiple options for students to record key ideas with Choice Note-Taking, allowing students to select independent learning tasks from activity Choice Boards, and supporting interest-based research mini-projects with Spin-Offs are all ways to help students become more engaged and invested in their work—and take responsibility for their own learning.

■ CHOICE HOMEWORK

Many teachers find, as I have, that students in the middle to upper grades frequently resist doing homework. While most students are capable of doing the work, some simply choose not to do it. They report lack of interest in doing what they perceive to be "busy work." Homework seems repetitive and boring to them. There is little motivation to complete the assignment other than to get credit for doing it. To combat this lack of interest, I have used **Choice Homework** with great success. Teachers report a marked increase in the turn-in rate. Students exhibit great enthusiasm on Choice Homework nights.

Ideally, you should offer a balance between types of homework that require left-hemispheric processing (focusing on analytical and sequential activities, including reading and writing) and types that require right-hemispheric processing (focusing on problem solving and unstructured and creative activities, including visual and spatial processing) (Contine, 1995). Over time, such a balance reinforces preferred learning styles and strengthens less-preferred learning styles for all students. In fact, when you make choices about which activities to present, consider activities that engage both hemispheres (writing about a political cartoon or writing a summary of conclusions after looking at a graph), which help the brain integrate information more easily.

While it's tempting to just give students a list of homework choices, it is very important to model each choice, one at a time. Discuss "what quality looks like" by identifying with your students the attributes of a well-done assignment. Your list might include neatness, completeness, details to support ideas, accuracy, and creativity.

When you're convinced that students understand what quality looks like in a particular homework choice, you can add an extra choice and begin the modeling process once again. Over subsequent weeks, you should continue to model and provide guided practice for new activities, slowly adding to the list of independent choices.

Choice Homework night becomes something that most students look

When we were studying fractions, I decided to try Choice Homework. I based the choices on different multiple intelligences. The response from the kids was terrific. I'll definitely offer Choice Homework again!

Here are some homework choices that worked for us:

- Use manipulatives, fraction pieces, or fraction strips to solve the fraction problems. (bodily-kinesthetic)
- Draw pictures to solve the problems. (spatial)
- Use paper and pencil to solve the problems. (logical-mathematical)
- Use the computer. Visit a teacher-selected Web site. Solve the fraction problems. (logical-mathematical)

—CAROLE KREISBERG
FIFTH-GRADE TEACHER

When presenting students with Choice Homework options, it's important to include a cross-section of multiple intelligence–based choices in order to address their diverse learning styles. Also consider including both logical/analytical activities, as well as creative, open-ended activities.

forward to. For that reason, I recommend keeping it novel by offering it once every week or two. As so many teachers have reported, the enthusiasm for doing homework is never higher than when students are offered homework options that appeal to their interests and strengths.

Figure 3.1 provides options for Choice Homework night that offer students a variety of multiple intelligence–based activities for making sense of the key ideas in their reading assignments.

Figure 3.1

CHOICE HOMEWORK OPTIONS
for finding key ideas in a reading assignment

Along with tonight's reading assignment, choose one of the following:

- **Complete a set of notes/make an outline** of the key ideas.
- **Create a set of five newspaper headlines** representing key ideas.
- **Draw three pictures (with captions)** that illustrate three important ideas.
- **Create a visual timeline (with captions)** to highlight key events.
- **Find 25 to 30 important words or phrases** in the reading. Group the terms and create your own Concept Map or graphic organizer to illustrate your understanding of the reading.
- **Rewrite the reading as a newspaper article.** Using the 5 W's, include details to support your main ideas.
- **Create a top-ten list** of things you should understand about the reading. Prepare the list on an overhead transparency to present to your peers.
- **Visit a teacher-recommended Web site** and summarize your findings.
- **Opt for a Spin-Off** (an independent, mini-research project based on your particular interest in the topic). Include main ideas and details.
- **Create a Net-Knowledge Page** by using the Internet to gather hyperlinks for URLs of Web sites related to the topic, key ideas, and images to support your reading.

Don't feel you have to grade or go over every student's homework on Choice Homework night. Instead, allow students to share in groups for a few minutes and use a simple assessment for self-evaluation or peer-evaluation. This assessment may take the form of a checklist enumerating each task required or a rubric with a work quality rating and a cooperation rating (see Figure 3.2.). Over the course of the week, you might invite a few students to share their homework with the whole class. Remember, the purpose of this activity is motivation and the opportunity for students to do something they might not get to do during class.

CHOICE HOMEWORK NIGHT ASSESSMENT

SELF-EVALUATION / PEER-EVALUATION

Your Name: Mandy Partner's Name Carmen

Circle **I** for self-evaluation/Circle **my partner** for peer-evaluation:

It was evident that I / (my partner) completed the task carefully. **Comment**: Her poster "British Actions" was neat + creative. She put a tea bag on it to show Americans couldn't import tea accept from England.

On a scale of 1 to 4 (4 is the highest), how would you rate the following:

I / (My partner) **identified key ideas** in the homework. Circle one: 1 2 3 (4)

I / (My partner) **gave details** to support the key ideas. Circle one: 1 2 (3) ~~4~~

One thing I / (my partner) could have done better was: include the Quartering Act

Choice Activity: Newspaper Headlines

One of my favorite social studies Choice Homework activities is writing newspaper headlines. This activity helps students to summarize key ideas. Here's how to make it work: Bring in several newspapers with headlines you've highlighted to illustrate how headlines convey important information in a succinct manner. For independent practice, select appropriately leveled articles from a newspaper or magazine for kids, put students into small groups, hand each group an article without a headline, and ask them to come up with a headline for the article. When students grasp how to cull information to create short, informative headlines, read aloud one section from a social studies or science textbook, and model how you would write newspaper headlines to demonstrate your understanding of the key ideas. Encourage the class to brainstorm on the board as many headlines for the chapter section as possible. Finally, discuss which five headlines would be most important to keep and which ones might be eliminated if you were trying to highlight the key understandings of the reading. This discussion

TIP

Be sure to provide linguistic formats of note-taking (Column Note-Taking, Noting What I've Learned, and Dialectical Journals) as well as graphic formats (Visual Text Notes), to appeal to a broad range of learners.

also helps build note-taking skills as students decide which information is most important to remember (or record), and which is less important.

For class practice, ask students to read another section of the textbook, and individually, or in pairs, have them write two or three new headlines. For homework, assign new readings, once again, with the goal of creating effective headlines to highlight key understandings. Depending upon the age and readiness of your students, you might continue to offer guided practice with this homework option, before adding it to your list of independent homework choices.

■ CHOICE NOTE-TAKING

Most teachers agree that taking notes is a critical skill that students must master to be successful in school. Since most students are visual learners, their need to write down summaries, key ideas, and symbols in a notebook is critical to retaining information. Too often, however, the only practice students get with note-taking is copying their teachers' notes off the board. Since students' organizational skills and ability to function independently vary greatly in a mixed-readiness classroom, you need to begin note-taking instruction with a very basic note-taking format and provide multiple guided-practice opportunities for using it, in class and with partners, before assigning independent practice. Begin to offer alternative strategies and less-structured formats as you notice that some students can take notes more independently.

Since no two students are alike, it is essential to provide options for note-taking that will appeal to different types of learners. I have seen teachers struggle to teach traditional outlining to students who are not yet developmentally ready to use a strategy requiring such complex organizational skills. Most of these students, while providing organized notes when under their teachers' structured guidance, never make the transfer to independent note-taking using traditional outlining. Instead, I offer several alternatives that are easy to use with students in elementary and middle school and beyond. Column Note-Taking and Noting What I've Learned are structured formats for beginning note-taking. Dialectical Journals and Visual Note-Taking are open-ended strategies that will appeal to more independent learners and divergent thinkers.

My favorite note-taking strategy is **Column Note-Taking**, which I adapted from the Cornell note-taking system, developed at Cornell University more than 40 years ago (Pauk, 1997). This system was originally developed for college students, but I have modified it for younger students. When you use this activity with students, have them read or listen to a short passage or brief lecture and ask them to record details in the right-hand Note Column of the two-column page (see Figure 3.3).

Figure 3.3

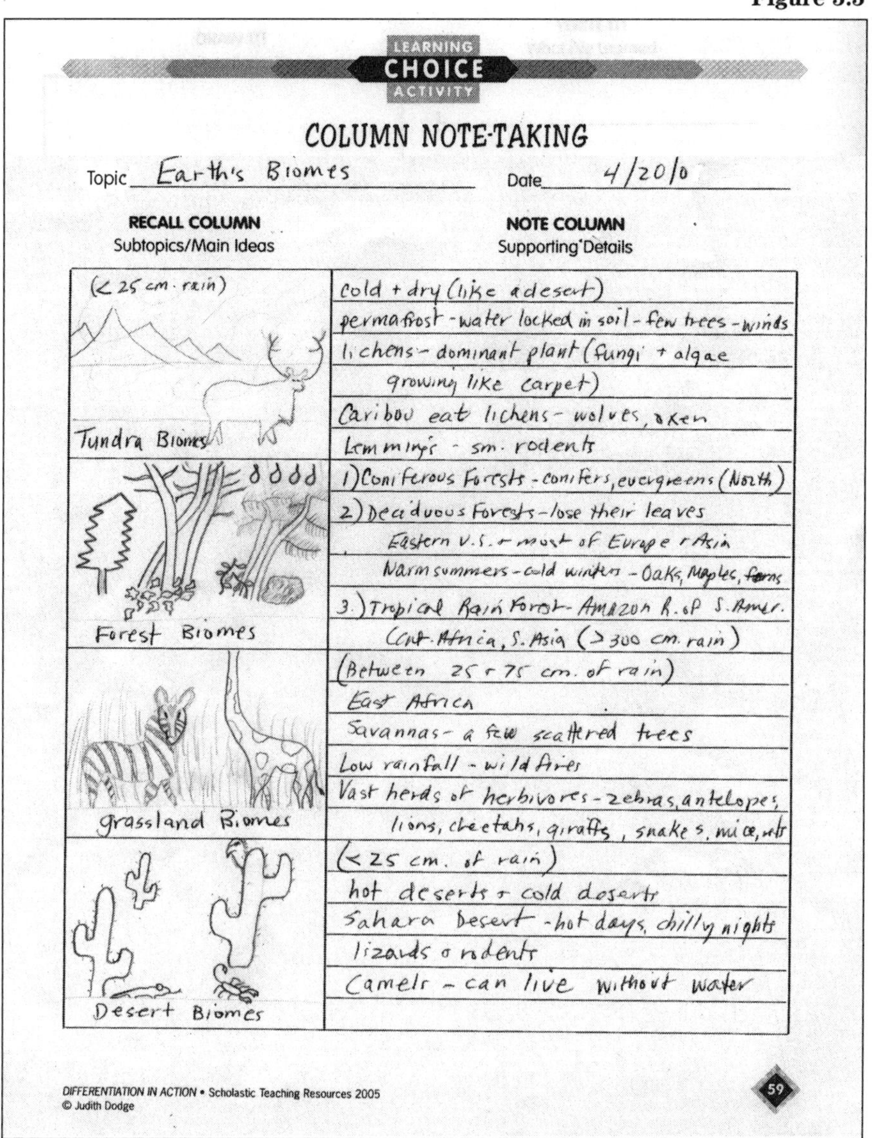

LEARNING CHOICE ACTIVITY

COLUMN NOTE-TAKING

Topic Earth's Biomes Date 4/20/0

RECALL COLUMN Subtopics/Main Ideas	NOTE COLUMN Supporting Details
(< 25 cm. rain) Tundra Biomes	cold + dry (like a desert) permafrost - water locked in soil - few trees - winds lichens - dominant plant (fungi + algae growing like carpet) Caribou eat lichens - wolves, oxen Lemmings - sm. rodents
Forest Biomes	1) Coniferous Forests - conifers, evergreens (North) 2) Deciduous Forests - lose their leaves Eastern U.S. + most of Europe + Asia Warm summers - cold winters - Oaks, Maples, ferns 3.) Tropical Rain Forest - Amazon R. of S. Amer. Cnt. Africa, S. Asia (> 300 cm. rain)
Grassland Biomes	(Between 25 + 75 cm. of rain) East Africa Savannas - a few scattered trees Low rainfall - wild fires Vast herds of herbivores - zebras, antelopes, lions, cheetahs, giraffs, snakes, mice, rats
Desert Biomes	(< 25 cm. of rain) hot deserts + cold deserts Sahara Desert - hot days, chilly nights lizards + rodents Camels - can live without water

DIFFERENTIATION IN ACTION • Scholastic Teaching Resources 2005
© Judith Dodge

59

Students using Column Note-Taking record details in the Note Column and a main idea and drawing in the Recall Column.

Then, provide a few minutes for students to reread their notes, reflect, and form questions, write comments, or note key ideas in the left-hand Recall Column. Encourage them, also, to draw symbols and pictures in the left-column boxes to help make the information memorable. You might want to introduce this strategy by having students fill out copies of the reproducible Column Note-Taking form on page 59. Once they're familiar with the activity, students can simply draw columns and rows in their notebooks or on a blank sheet of paper to recreate this note-taking format.

Used with students in younger grades, struggling learners, or students new to note-taking, **Noting What I've Learned** provides a simplified version of Column Note-Taking (Dodge, 1994). It offers greater structure by prompting students to provide three details for every main idea noted. As they draw the main idea in each box and write its three details, they create pre-writing material for an essay. Following this structured, visual format guides students to develop logical, coherent writing (see Figure 3.4). You can make copies of this format using the reproducible form on page 60 or have students create their own copy by drawing lines (or folding the paper) to create two columns and four rows.

Figure 3.4

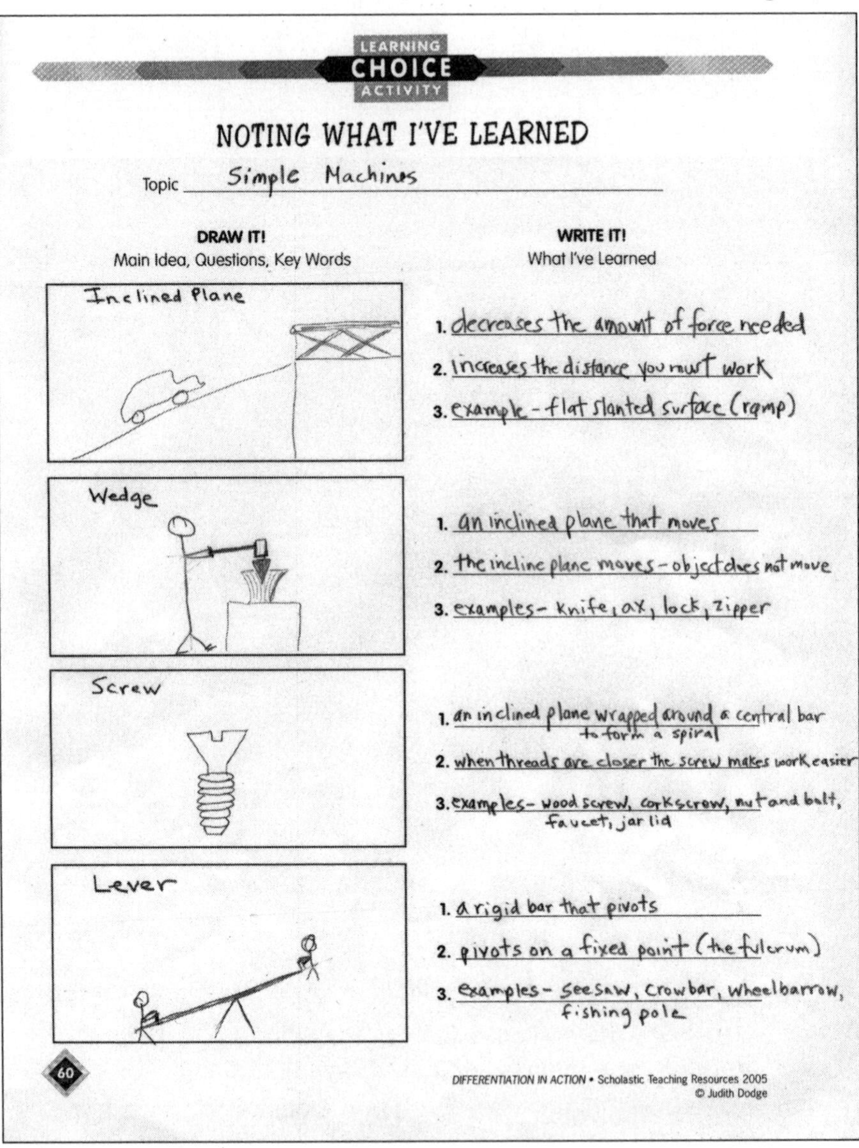

LEARNING CHOICE ACTIVITY

NOTING WHAT I'VE LEARNED

Topic Simple Machines

DRAW IT! Main Idea, Questions, Key Words	WRITE IT! What I've Learned
Inclined Plane	1. decreases the amount of force needed 2. increases the distance you must work 3. example - flat slanted surface (ramp)
Wedge	1. an inclined plane that moves 2. the incline plane moves - object does not move 3. examples - knife, ax, lock, zipper
Screw	1. an inclined plane wrapped around a central bar to form a spiral 2. when threads are closer the screw makes work easier 3. examples - wood screw, corkscrew, nut and bolt, faucet, jar lid
Lever	1. a rigid bar that pivots 2. pivots on a fixed point (the fulcrum) 3. examples - seesaw, crowbar, wheelbarrow, fishing pole

60

DIFFERENTIATION IN ACTION • Scholastic Teaching Resources 2005
© Judith Dodge

Students break down the topic "Simple Machines" into four subtopics with details.

Both strategies provide excellent study tools for students. Folding the page to cover the right column, students can quiz themselves by reciting information triggered by questions or notes in the left column. Uncovering their notes, they can get immediate feedback about the accuracy and completeness of their answers.

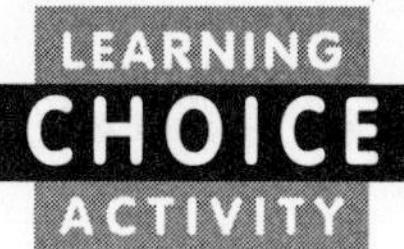

COLUMN NOTE-TAKING

Topic ______________________________ Date ____________________

RECALL COLUMN Subtopics/Main Ideas	**NOTE COLUMN** Supporting Details

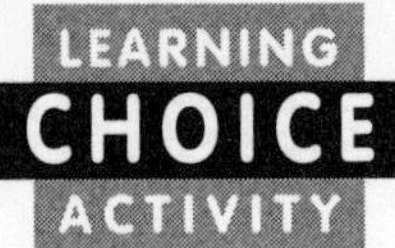

NOTING WHAT I'VE LEARNED

Topic ______________________________

DRAW IT!
Main Idea, Questions, Key Words

WRITE IT!
What I've Learned

1. ______________________________
2. ______________________________
3. ______________________________

1. ______________________________
2. ______________________________
3. ______________________________

1. ______________________________
2. ______________________________
3. ______________________________

1. ______________________________
2. ______________________________
3. ______________________________

Another excellent note-taking strategy is the **Dialectical Journal.** Designed to engage students as active readers, this two-column format promotes students' critical thinking. It encourages students to pick out important phrases, quotes, and key ideas from their reading and asks them to reflect on and react to these selections from the text. This interaction helps students to make sense of what they read and to find personal relevance in the selection—responses that in turn promote comprehension and retention of information.

Because of the open-ended nature of the task (students can choose to respond in any way they want), students of all readiness levels in reading can complete a Dialectical Journal. With struggling readers, you might provide or highlight particular sections of text and offer a prompt (*I agree with the author because. . . . I think this quote means . . .*) to help start them off with a response.

Introduce this strategy while you are reading an information-rich passage with your class. Distribute copies of the reproducible form on page 63 or simply have students fold a page in half lengthwise to create a two-column format. Draw your own format on the chalkboard or use a copy on an overhead transparency. Do a Think Aloud with students as you choose a fact, statement, phrase, or quote to record in the left column. Show students how you reflect, react, or comment upon what you have recorded by noting a connection, giving an opinion with supporting evidence, or making a prediction in the right column. Continue reading with students and pausing to let them make their own notes. Provide guided independent practice in class so students can see the variety of reactions, connections, and responses that are possible. Then, give students independent practice with the strategy by assigning the Dialectical Journal with readings for homework. For ideas and prompts, see Figure 3.5, Using Dialectical Journals to Take Notes, on page 62.

You can provide repeated opportunities for practicing this type of note-taking by assigning it for each section of a given chapter in a novel or a social studies or science textbook. You may want to offer students a choice of Column Note-Taking or Dialectical Journals for a subsequent chapter. Then, return to multiple opportunities for Dialectical Journaling in the following chapter. This variation will provide an appropriate balance between teacher direction and student choice for learners in processing activities.

Moving from linguistic formats of note-taking to a more graphic format, you can introduce your students to **Visual Text Notes**. Your visual and spatial learners will appreciate this choice of note-taking—it allows and encourages them to draw pictures and symbols to help make information memorable.

Figure 3.5

Using Dialectical Journals to Take Notes

Dialectical Journals promote critical thinking while engaging students to interact with fiction or nonfiction text.

Student records:	Student reflects on and reacts to the selected part of the text:
(FICTION OR NONFICTION) • A key passage • A phrase from text or poem	*This reminds me of. . .* (Make a personal connection, a connection to another text, or a connection to the real world. Explain.) *I think this means. . .* *I think this is significant because. . .* *This is mostly about. . .*
(FICTION OR NONFICTION) • What the author says	*I believe. . . because. . . (support with evidence)* *I agree/disagree because. . .* *The author's viewpoint. . .* *The purpose of this reading is to. . .*
(FICTION) • A character's words/quotes • An action taken by a character • What others say about the character	Describe what the words or actions tell you about the character. How do you feel about what the character says or does? *I predict that. . .* *This makes me feel that the character. . .*
(NONFICTION) • Notes • Main ideas • Key concepts • Important events • Key facts • Sequence of steps	Write a reaction or comment that analyzes, compares or contrasts, evaluates, or judges the information. Create a metaphor for the information. (____ is like ____.) *This is like/This is different from. . . because. . .* *The sequence is important because. . .* *It would be better if. . .* *A different solution might have been. . .* *This is important to know/remember because. . .*
(NONFICTION) • Descriptive notes on a *primary source* document (For example: *Political cartoon, speech, song, diary entry, chart, table, graph, map)*	What does it refers to/What does it mean? What does it tell you about the time period, culture, people, or event? What outside information can you relate through prior knowledge?

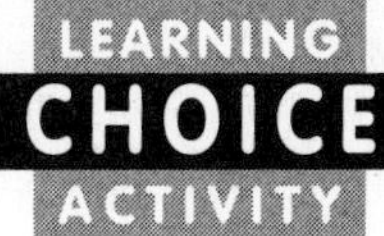

USING DIALECTICAL JOURNALS TO TAKE NOTES

In this column, record...

- a passage
- a phrase
- a quote
- a main idea
- an important event
- a key fact
- a name of document
- anything you feel is important

In this column...

- Write a reaction
- Discuss the significance
- Make a connection
- Make a comparison
- Evaluate/Judge an idea
- Predict a future outcome
- Reflect in any other way that is meaningful to you

KEY IDEA

Alternating between left- and right-brain activities by providing different kinds of note-taking formats will help students integrate information more readily and retain it longer.

Provide students with a note-taking page divided into eight boxes and ask them to use each box to highlight a key understanding or concept they learned from the reading. Encourage them to sketch pictures and create nonlinguistic representations to help make the information memorable. Tell them to include key vocabulary and necessary terms to add meaning to the drawings. At first, you will want to remain very structured, and you may even provide students with the eight concepts to take notes on. You could write key terms on the board or fill in the note-taking page with terms and then photocopy it. To challenge individual students, you could allow them to read and take notes without this support. Eventually, however, you will want to make this activity more open-ended for all students, letting them decide independently which concepts should be noted. The resulting notes with images will serve as an excellent study tool later on.

Be sure to spend enough time modeling each of the strategies above before moving on to a new note-taking method. Once students are comfortable with more than one strategy, allow them many opportunities to choose

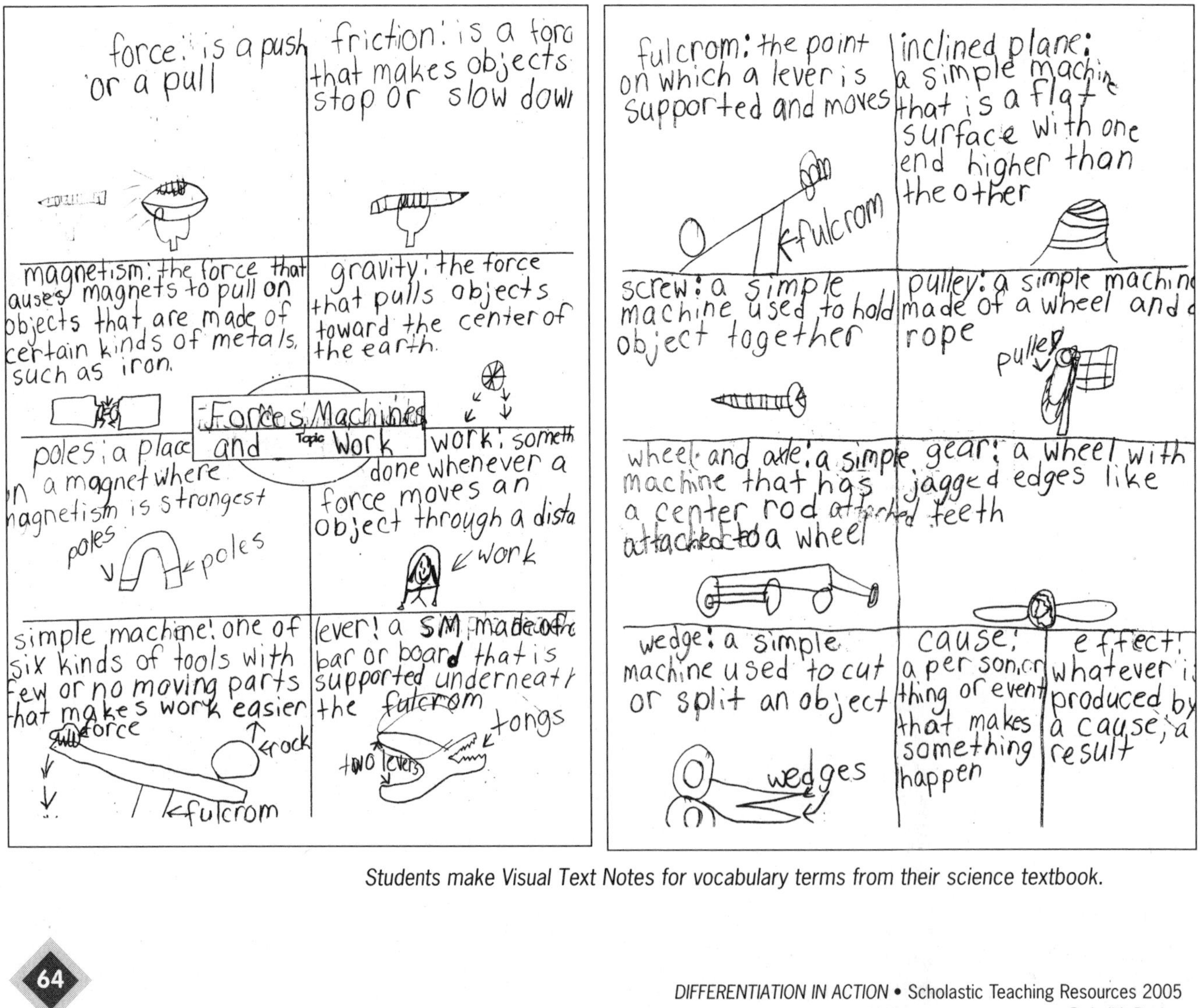

Students make Visual Text Notes for vocabulary terms from their science textbook.

which note-taking strategy they would like to use during a particular class discussion or homework reading assignment.

■ CHOICE BOARDS

After reading a novel with the entire class, teachers will frequently assign one project for all students to complete in order to synthesize their learning. They might assign all students to write an epilogue to a story, using what they know and understand to predict the future of the characters.

Imagine the excitement you would feel as a student if, instead, you were given several follow-up options to choose from. If you love to write creatively, you may choose the epilogue. If you excel at drawing, you may choose to write a PhotoJournal combining your love of drawing with the task of writing about change over time in the main character. If you are a tactile learner, you may prefer to create a PowerPoint presentation showing evidence of the character's attributes from his actions in the story.

Choice Boards are menus of learning tasks that provide multiple options for student learning or assessment. Like Choice Homework, they generate enthusiasm for learning and intrinsic motivation. Keep in mind that there are as many ways to use Choice Boards as there are ways to design them. I have worked with teachers to develop Choice Boards organized around learning styles to allow students to work in the way they learn best (see Figure 3.6: A Learning Styles Choice Board), around multiple intelligences to motivate learners (see Figure 3.7: A Multiple Intelligence–Based Choice Board) and around levels of Bloom's Taxonomy to challenge levels of thinking (see Figure 3.8: A Bloom Choice Board). They can be used for homework, class activities, or end-of-unit products.

You can also design Choice Boards around any aspect of the curriculum from developing skills (writing, spelling, vocabulary, and math) to processing information (making meaning and improving comprehension) to synthesizing and reflecting upon key understandings about a topic or novel at the end of a unit (the Industrial Revolution, *Tales of a Fourth Grade Nothing*, the planets, taking a trip to Mexico). They can be generic to a discipline or specific to a topic or concept (see Figure 3.9: Immigration Choice Board [Social Studies]).

If you choose to design a Choice Board on a specific topic, novel, or unit, it is important to first consider and list key concepts for understanding. Then, as you plan the choices, you can make sure that the essential understandings drive the options you develop—that the assessment is aligned with the curriculum.

With thoughtful planning, you can tier some of the activities, providing for multiple levels of challenge within one option. For example, instead of having a student write a postcard back home to a friend describing the new life he or she found as an immigrant to America, an advanced learner could be asked to compare and contrast in at least three ways the life in the

One of the ways I like to use the Choice Boards is to give each child a copy to put in his homework folder. Then, on a particular night, if a student finds the homework is too easy, or too hard, he can choose an alternative homework task to complete for credit. I also offer the Choice Board as extra credit and to challenge advanced learners.

—C. SANTOMAURO
MANHASSET SCHOOLS

A teacher who is attempting to teach without inspiring the pupil with a desire to learn is hammering on a cold iron.
HORACE MANN

country he or she left behind with the new life found in America. The comparison makes the activity more complex, engaging higher levels of thinking. (For a more detailed discussion of tiering assignments, see Chapter 7.)

You can individualize learning tasks for students with different levels of readiness by assigning them tasks related to their needs. You may want to assign some tasks that all students complete and allow students to choose from one or more other options on the board. Or you can assign students to choose options from a particular row of leveled options on the board. Invite students to occasionally create their own activity, helping them to integrate information or use it in new and original ways.

The trick is not to overwhelm your students with too many choices. Depending upon the age, readiness, and independence of your students, you can choose to use a Four-Box, Six-Box, or Nine-Box Choice Board. The complexity of the tasks and the time needed to complete them will determine how many you assign. A reproducible Nine-Box Choice Board template is provided on page 70.

When you assign activities in the Choice Board format, you can place the options on index cards in pockets on a bulletin board. By doing so, you create a permanent center for Choice Boards, and you can change the option cards within the pockets for every unit or topic. Sometimes I like to hand out a menu of choices to each student at the beginning or middle of a unit, providing students with multiple opportunities for using them over time. At other times, I have given the Choice Board out at the end of the unit for a one-time choice of synthesis activity or alternative assessment.

Don't be overly concerned if you notice that some students tend to do the same type of activity whenever they are given a choice (for example, a student who loves to draw will frequently choose that same option). This is not surprising, when we consider that one of the purposes of providing options is to give learners exactly what they prefer so they are intrinsically motivated to show-what-they-know in the best way they can. You can, however, set a goal with kids to try different options from the Choice Board, from time to time, to strengthen weaker areas of development.

Still, if you're not comfortable with students frequently choosing the same option, you can allow students to choose and repeat their favorite option once and then require they try something new. You can provide students with a checklist to keep track of their choices over time.

However they are used, Choice Boards are a sure way to engage learners in sense-making tasks that address their individual strengths, talents, and needs.

Figure 3.6

A Learning Styles Choice Board

CHOICES TO ADDRESS PREFERENCES IN LEARNING STYLES

Choose an activity below to help you make sense of the information we are studying.

Topic/Concept: ______________________________

Auditory Activities	Visual Activities	Tactile-Kinesthetic Activities
• Teach a lesson	• Create a Web site	• Gather an Artifact Box
• Give a speech	• Create a PhotoJournal	• Give a demonstration
• Prepare/gather recordings	• Prepare a PowerPoint presentation	• Present a TV newscast
• Conduct an interview	• Design an advertisement or poster	• Make a videotape
• Listen to a tape	• Design a graphic organizer	• Play or create a game
• Be part of a panel	• Create/gather a gallery of pictures	• Sort, group, and categorize a collection
• Engage in a debate	• Chart a visual timeline	• Role-play with props

Figure 3.7

A Multiple Intelligence–Based Choice Board

CHOICES FOR MAKING SENSE OF INFORMATION

Choose an activity below to help you make sense of the information we are studying.

Topic/Concept: ______________________________

Select key ideas in this lesson to present in a NewsFlash! (Interpersonal)	**Organize this information in a chart or graphic organizer.** (Logical-Mathematical)
Draw or illustrate the main ideas. (Spatial)	**Summarize the key ideas by creating two headlines you might see in the newspaper.** (Verbal-Linguistic)

Figure 3.8

A Bloom Choice Board

CHOICES AT SIX LEVELS OF BLOOM'S TAXONOMY

Choose one activity from each level below to help you make sense of the information we are studying.

Topic/Concept: ______________________________

Knowledge Level: • *Recall* the story/events. • *List* the facts. • *Define* the terms. • *Label* the parts. • *Name* the locations/types of. . .	**Analysis Level:** • *Sequence* steps or events. • *Organize* the information into a chart or graphic organizer. • *Group, sort, and categorize* the information. • *Compare and contrast.* • *Differentiate or distinguish.*
Comprehension Level: • *Explain* the procedure, event, concept. • *Describe* what this is mostly about. (What is main idea?) • *Paraphrase* what you heard/read	**Synthesis Level:** • *Design/invent/compose/create* something new. • *Propose an alternative solution/ending.* • *Suggest* what would happen if. . . ? • *Combine ideas* to propose something new.
Application Level: • *Demonstrate or illustrate* this information. • *Give* some examples. • *Solve...* • *Use* the rule, formula, or principle learned. • *Construct* a model to show your understanding of. . .	**Evaluation Level:** • *Judge* the importance. • *Evaluate* which is the best/worst/most important/least important. • *Prioritize/rate in order.* • *Recommend.* • *Agree or disagree.*

Figure 3.9

Immigration Choice Board (Social Studies)

Key Understandings:
- Where did American immigrants come from?
- Why did immigrants leave their countries?
- What obstacles did immigrants face when they arrived in America?

Put on a skit Dress up as an immigrant. Talk about the journey on the ship coming across the ocean. Be sure to talk about the reasons you left, the difficulties of your journey, and your excitement about the future. *(Bodily-Kinesthetic)*	**Draw a poster** Compare and contrast the geography and occupations of the country you came from with those of your new country. *(Spatial)*	**Write a Poem** Imagine you are an immigrant in America. Write a poem about why you left your old country or about your new life in America. Be sure to include adjectives and verbs. *(Musical)*
Pack a suitcase Put in items you would take with you to remember your old country. Include a diary with at least two entries about your journey and hopes for the future. *(Bodily-Kinesthetic)*	**Teach a game** Research games played in the country from which you emigrated. Choose one to teach to the class. *(Bodily-Kinesthetic/ Interpersonal)*	**Make a graph** Interview school staff and classmates to learn about where people emigrated from. Create a graph. Write at least two observations. *(Interpersonal/Logical-Mathematical)*
Write a postcard Write a postcard to a friend or family member who stayed behind. Tell about your journey, your new home, your father's new work, your present living conditions. *(Verbal-Linguistic/Intrapersonal)*	**Learn a song** Research a patriotic song either from the country you left or from your new country. Learn it and share it with the class. *(Musical)*	**Create a diorama** Create a diorama showing what you would see coming into New York harbor. Examples: Statue of Liberty, Ellis Island, harbor, American flag, New York skyline, other boats filled with immigrants. Include a caption describing the importance of each. *(Spatial)*

LONG BEACH TEACHERS

LEARNING

NINE-BOX CHOICE BOARD

ACTIVITY

Topic: ______________________________

Key Understandings:
- ______________________________
- ______________________________
- ______________________________

MI:	MI:	MI:
MI:	**Your Choice** (check your idea with your teacher first) MI:	MI:
MI:	MI:	MI:

Key to Multiple Intelligences:

V Verbal-linguistic
L Logical-mathematical
S Spatial
B Bodily-kinesthetic
M Musical
I Interpersonal
A Intrapersonal
N Naturalist

■ SPIN-OFFS

I remember when my younger son was in third grade and his teacher declared him and his classmates to be "researchers" and "explorers." Each child received a clipboard and had access to an array of resources in the classroom, including tables of teacher-gathered materials, nonfiction books and magazines, and computers. When we visited his classroom, my son discussed with pride all the topics he had explored as a researcher. That was when I first recognized the benefits of short, mini-research explorations. He showed me around the room and shared with me what he had discovered. Instead of completing one major report requiring months of research, organization, and independence, he had learned how to find information about a range of topics by being given numerous brief opportunities to practice necessary skills. He had learned to search nonfiction text for key ideas and to take notes so he could present a brief written summary report on these topics.

Carol Ann Tomlinson, in *The Differentiated Classroom: Responding to the Needs of All Learners* (1999), discusses how important it is that teachers provide multiple opportunities for students to engage in independent study. She suggests that teachers should systematically aid students in developing curiosity, pursuing topics that interest them, developing plans to find answers to their intriguing questions, managing time, setting goals and criteria for work, assessing their progress, presenting new understandings to audiences who can appreciate them—and beginning the cycle again. By using Spin-Off projects wisely, teachers can address many of those goals.

Spin-Offs are projects based on student interest (Heacox, 2002). Because students choose their own topics, they become more fully engaged in the process of learning. When struggling learners choose topics of personal relevance, they often become surprisingly resourceful at locating information. Advanced learners finally have the opportunity to break away from the rest of the class and explore something in great depth that intrigues them.

Spin-Off projects can be done individually or with a partner. The next time one of your students raises a question about a subject you will never get to cover in class, encourage him or her to do a Spin-Off. The next time someone raises a topic that is tangential to your discussion, add it to a class list of potential Spin-Off topics to be studied independently. Instead of assigning the whole class a topic for a report or project at the end of a unit of study, allow each student to choose a Spin-Off that intrigues them.

I have no special talent. I am only passionately curious.

ALBERT EINSTEIN

RELATED LITERATURE

Read more about Spin-Offs in Diane Heacox's book: *Differentiating Instruction in the Regular Classroom* (Free Spirit Publishing, 2002).

KEY IDEA

Spin-Offs cultivate curiosity as students pursue topics of interest. They also provide opportunities for students to develop independent work skills.

TIP

You can provide Spin-Offs as a homework option on Choice Homework night, as an end-of-unit project to encourage pursuit of new knowledge, or as an extra-credit option for eager learners.

It is important to remember, however, that students vary in their readiness for independence. Therefore, Spin-Offs must be thoughtfully planned so that students move toward greater independence gradually. I recommend holding 10- to 15-minute mini-lesson workshops for the whole class to teach key research and independent-work skills: how to narrow down a topic, where to find information, how to use different resources, how to set appropriate work goals and manage time, and how to present information in different ways. Subsequently, you can gather students in flexible groups to work on areas of need as they arise. Periodically, set aside class time for students to work on their Spin-Offs. The length of time spent on a Spin-Off can vary, from one evening or class period to several. Allow students additional time at home, if needed, to finish their Spin-Off.

In addition to mini-lesson instruction, you can support students with a Project Planner that includes due dates, a self-evaluation, and a work log. Provide students with copies of the Project Planner on page 74 and review short-term due dates for choosing a topic, developing questions to explore, completing notes, visuals, a self-evaluation, and the presentation itself. Have students complete the self-evaluation before they present their information to judge how accurately they followed directions for this independent project.

As described by Diane Heacox, there are three types of Spin-Offs: a teacher-directed Spin-Off, a Spin-Off with a required product, and a student-directed Spin-Off. An example of a teacher-directed Spin-Off would be a class author study that allows each student to choose his or her own author, but requires all students to include certain content or key ideas (the author's childhood, factors affecting the author's writing, key people who influenced the author's writing, the author's style, examples of the author's books). Students also may choose how they want to present what they have learned. (See A Multiple Intelligence–Based Product List in Chapter 5 for ideas students can choose from.)

A Spin-Off with a required product could be a mini-project in which students choose their own topics and the content or key ideas they'll include, while you assign the product all students must deliver. A three-minute "how-to" oral report, for which each student chooses his or her own topic, would be such an example.

A student-directed Spin-Off provides the most independence, allowing students to choose their own topic, content, and product. Students who are used to doing independent work will find this open, flexible format easier to manage than students new to such research. Student-directed Spin-Offs may particularly appeal to those students who need more of a challenge, providing them with more open-endedness and independence.

When all of my students are engaged in Spin-Offs, I assess what they've learned through their oral presentation or the poster they present. When individuals work on a Spin-Off for extra credit or as a homework option, however, I need a quick way to check and assess their work. On these occasions, I use the Concept Summary handout on page 75. The "researchers" list key terms they've learned, draw a picture that visually summarizes their learning, and write a brief paragraph that does the same. The Concept Summary is easy for me to check (I can even take it home with me to grade), and I can quickly glean what my students have learned.

Alternating among the three Spin-Off options will contribute to the balance of teacher direction and student centeredness that you want to achieve in a differentiated classroom. These mini-projects provide structure as well as offering flexibility so you can reach a range of students' abilities.

By now you're familiar with ways to ensure that intrinsic motivation is a driving force in your instruction. Granting students a variety of choices on a regular basis creates conditions under which students want to learn. By caring enough to offer students activities that make them comfortable, as well as appropriately challenge them, we are able to embrace the range of learners that sit every day in our multi-ability classrooms.

In the next chapter we take a closer look at the choices you provide for students and evaluate these choices based on their rigor and complexity. Providing choices is not enough, in itself, to produce powerful learning. Providing choices that *evoke critical thinking* makes all the difference.

LONG-TERM PROJECT PLANNER

For each task you complete, put a check mark in the appropriate box.

❒ Due date for choosing topic and questions: ______________________________

My topic: ____

Questions to explore:

____

____

____

____

❒ Due date for notes: ______________________

❒ Due date for visual(s): ______________________

❒ Due date for self-evaluation: ______________________

❒ Due date for presentation: ______________________

How will you share your information? Circle one:

Giving an oral presentation/Making a display or poster

Self-Evaluation

❒ My information is accurate.

❒ My information includes key ideas about my topic.

❒ My visual supports my new understandings.

❒ I have used **at least** three varied sources. They are:

____

____

____

CONCEPT SUMMARY

Topic ____

Draw a picture or write symbols in this box to summarize the topic.

List key words about the topic.

Paragraph: ***Summarize*** your learning by using as many of the key words as you can. Do not simply give definitions of the terms. Use them in sentences that show you understand their meanings. ***Check off*** terms above, as you use them. ***Circle*** terms below, in your writing.

PRINCIPLES OF EFFECTIVE INSTRUCTION EXPLORED IN THIS CHAPTER:

Ongoing and frequent assessments

•

The use of brain research

•

Organizing learning around the "big ideas"

•

Scaffolding

•

Challenging Options

•

Tiering

CHAPTER 4

Differentiating Instruction Using Bloom's Taxonomy

Every teacher remembers having studied Bloom's Taxonomy in some education course. For many of us, that distant lesson sounds familiar but may not have greatly impacted our daily lesson planning. Somewhere in the back of our minds we know that Bloom identified six levels of complexity of human thought: *knowledge*, *comprehension*, *application*, *analysis*, *synthesis*, *evaluation* (Bloom, 1956). We briefly studied the critical thinking skills engaged at each level but then put aside the focus on process to concentrate on *covering* the great deal of content we each found in our curriculum.

This chapter suggests that Bloom's Taxonomy remains a user-friendly, familiar model that can help teachers of all grade levels and subject areas to ask questions and design tasks that engage critical thinking and appropriately challenge students. When used consistently, the taxonomy can help students make a "quantum leap to higher order thinking" (Sousa, 2001).

Show Me the Research!

Recently, brain research has refocused our attention on *how the brain learns* content and has reminded us that thinking is the process humans use to collect information about the world and organize it in a personally meaningful way. To learn content, we observe, find patterns and generalize, form conclusions based on patterns, and assess conclusions based on observations (Sousa, 2001). Content taught in isolation, as facts without personal meaning or connections to other ideas, has little chance of being deeply understood or remembered. When we engage thinking skills—the process skills of reasoning, comparing, relating, judging, and the like—we make the content meaningful and relevant. We increase the likelihood that students remember the information.

We should be aware of a few problems that new research has brought to our attention regarding the taxonomy. Bloom and his colleagues attempted to use *degree of difficulty* as the basis for the difference between the levels. But in fact, the higher levels are not always more difficult (Costa, 2001). You have probably seen evidence of this yourself when you have asked a special-needs child to judge the value of something or to rate the best or worst in a category (the highest level of the taxonomy: evaluation) Most likely, he or she was able to give an opinion and support it with reasons. On the other hand, the student may have had more difficulty reading a passage and using it to analyze a character's attributes (a lower level on the taxonomy: analysis).

We must be careful not to assign more difficult tasks (tasks requiring more effort or time) when what we mean to do is challenge students with more rigorous tasks (tasks requiring more complex thought).

Sousa refers to this problem as well when he suggests that we need to pay attention to the difference between *difficulty* and *complexity* when designing learning tasks (2001). Unintentionally, many of us assign more *arduous* tasks (tasks requiring more effort or time) when what we mean to do is challenge students with more *rigorous* tasks (tasks requiring more-complex thought at high levels of Bloom's Taxonomy). Assigning an advanced student *two* paragraphs to write about an author's style instead of one (*increasing difficulty*) is not the same as assigning that student to write one paragraph that compares the author's style in one story to the style of a different author from a previously read story (*increasing complexity*).

Putting Research Into Practice

As teachers, we need to revisit Bloom's Taxonomy and apply our understanding of the different levels to curriculum design on a *daily* basis. Keep in mind that linking content to any of the process skills (relating, comparing, defending, sequencing, etc.) will help students understand and remember the content better. (See Figure 4.1 for a list of thinking/process skills involved at each level of Bloom's Taxonomy.) When we use powerful questioning techniques informed by the taxonomy, we engage student thinking and communication at a more rigorous level. The associations generated by more-complex thinking help the brain encode information in ways that make retrieval easier later on.

The best thing we can do to help students improve their comprehension through critical thinking is to teach them how to generate their *own* questions and thoughts at different levels. Richard and Jo Anne Vacca call this "active comprehension" (1996). Several teachers I have worked with have engaged their students in higher-level thinking by introducing them to the different levels of Bloom's Taxonomy. In one class, small groups worked to create questions and answers at each level for topics they had been studying. In another, the Bloom's Jeopardy games students designed helped them to review for tests in a way that assisted all levels of learners.

As we rediscover Bloom, we should keep a few things in mind. First, the levels are not necessarily sequential (Costa, 2001). In actual practice, constructing knowledge does not happen in a lockstep manner. In fact, constructivism often reverses the order of Bloom, beginning with an evaluative and analytical search for meaning and ending with comprehension and knowledge (Foote, Vermitte, & Battaglia, 2001). Second, the objectives at each level may overlap. It is not critical that students perform tasks at every level of the taxonomy. Many teachers in my workshops have struggled with deciding whether the questions and learning tasks they were creating were at a particular level. Through our exploration of the taxonomy, we've come to understand that instead of worrying about the exact level of a specific question or task, we should simply focus on making sure that the question or task elicits critical thinking (comparing, classifying, inferring, judging, and so forth). By asking students to identify assumptions and points of view, to examine and support their ideas, to demonstrate ideas in a new way, and to explore "what if" scenarios and alternative perspectives, we are assured of creating more-*complex* tasks that require higher-order thinking (Heacox, 2002; Wiggins, 2000). Any of those tasks would naturally elicit thought at higher levels of Bloom's Taxonomy and, certainly, prepare students for the rigors and type of thinking required on state assessments.

Slower learners can reach higher levels of Bloom's Taxonomy if we help them to focus on essential ideas and eliminate less important sublearnings.

(BLOOM, 1976; SOUSA, 2001).

I'm sure you have wondered at times whether or not you can bring students who are slower to process information up the taxonomy. In fact, slower learners can reach higher levels if we help them to focus on essential ideas and eliminate less important ones (Bloom, 1976; Sousa, 2001). While remembering all the details about a topic may be impossible for these learners, they do have the ability to compare and contrast, sort and distinguish, and judge and evaluate. Don't assume they are not capable of thinking critically because they take more time to master basic concepts. Instead, eliminate some of the details and focus on the big ideas and key concepts that all students must know and understand. By removing less important facts that would take these students more time to sort and classify, you allow them to concentrate on the main ideas. Under these scaffolded conditions, students often surprise us and perform at a higher level than we may expect.

Keeping in mind that students at all levels of cognitive ability can benefit from learning tasks leveled using Bloom's Taxonomy, what are some ways to use the taxonomy as a planning tool? I have compiled a few charts and activities that will help you examine, identify, and differentiate the challenge level of your questions and learning tasks.

Strategies

The following strategies employ Bloom's Taxonomy and can be integrated daily into your curriculum through discussion, guided practice, individual and group work, projects and homework assignments, and end-of-unit assessments. Using the Thinking in Bloom chart and the Question Starters will help you plan for activities and discussion questions with Bloom in mind. Assessments in Bloom will help you create alternative assessments based on a range of complexity and rigor. While all levels of the taxonomy are important, keep the focus on the higher levels of the taxonomy to ensure that students have the opportunity to process the content more deeply and more permanently. The questions and activities you provide at these levels will also help you differentiate by providing advanced learners opportunities for more divergent thinking.

■ THINKING IN BLOOM

The Thinking in Bloom chart (Figure 4.1) provides you with an overview of Bloom's Taxonomy, the thinking/process skills involved at each level of challenge, the action verbs used to describe tasks at each level, and several suggestions for designing show-what-you-know products. You'll notice that *synthesis*, rather that *evaluation*, is placed at the top of the taxonomy. Originally, Bloom presented *evaluation* as the level of his taxonomy that engages the most complex thinking. More recently, however, researchers have argued that synthesis (creating) involves more-complex thinking skills than does evaluation (critiquing) (Anderson & Krathwohl, 2001). I tend to agree with this interpretation, so I have reversed the highest two levels of the taxonomy in my chart. You can use this chart to help you design class activities, homework choices, and assessments that reflect rigorous thinking.

■ BLOOM QUESTION STARTERS

Bloom Question Starters are prompts for asking or writing questions at all levels of Bloom's Taxonomy. By asking students questions that move up the hierarchy, we invite them to examine information more deeply. Responding to questions at the higher levels requires making associations, noting relationships, and assessing conclusions. We differentiate our questioning in class when we ask learners who are at a more concrete stage questions at lower levels of the taxonomy, while we ask learners who are comfortable with abstract concepts questions at the higher levels. We must be sure not to ask questions in this way at all times, however, because we want to stretch the abilities of all students and invite them to demonstrate deeper understanding and to use the problem-solving skills at the higher levels. With this understanding in mind, we can use the Question Starters during class discussions to challenge students who have fully grasped a concept and, at the same time, begin to extend thinking for those students

Figure 4.1

THINKING IN BLOOM

Levels of Challenge	Thinking/Process Skills	Action Verbs	Products
Knowledge *Knowing*	Recalling, remembering, recognizing, identifying, defining	Tell, list, define, label, name, identify, match	Test, list, pictures, 5*W*'s, newspaper article, map, content-area dictionary
Comprehension *Understanding*	Interpreting, summarizing, explaining, describing, rewording, paraphrasing	Describe, explain, retell, discuss, summarize, interpret, paraphrase	T.V. bulletin, NewsFlash!, show and tell, oral report, visual with captions, chart
Application *Using*	Applying, selecting, transferring, relating, solving	Use, illustrate, locate information, research, show, demonstrate, perform, apply, solve, construct, compute	Set of newspaper headlines, report, illustration, journal entries, news story, pamphlet, timeline, simulation, teach a lesson, give a demonstration
Analysis *Breaking apart*	Analyzing, reasoning, distinguishing, comparing, contrasting, sequencing, noting relationships	Sort, group, classify, sequence, order, compare, contrast, note (causes, effects/advantages, disadvantages, etc.), categorize, separate	Collection, survey, questionnaire, graph, letter to the editor, a PowerPoint, chart, checklist, PhotoJournal, Artifact Box
Evaluation *Judging*	Judging, supporting, defending, criticizing, arguing, rating, prioritizing	Choose, support, justify, recommend, estimate, predict, assess, decide, prioritize, evaluate, rate, judge, critique	Top-ten list, "List of the best/worst...," book review, survey, debate, speech, awareness campaign, list of trends, editorial
Synthesis *Putting together in a new way*	Combining, creating, developing, rearranging, inferring, supposing, reorganizing, hypothesizing	Create, invent, design, compose, rewrite, formulate, develop, hypothesize	Invention, classified ad, campaign, action plan, game, poem, song, rap, experiment, slogan, advertisement, political cartoon

Based on Bloom, 1956

still struggling with the concepts. The Question Starters can also serve as prompts for written "checks for understanding" and reflections in JournalWrites, and for practice with extended response writing on state assessments.

To encourage students to use higher-level questions *themselves* during inquiry-based class discussions, hand out copies of the Question Starters on pages 82 and 83 for students to place in their notebooks. Allow students time to work with partners before the discussion begins, to develop several questions for each of the higher levels of Bloom's hierarchy. Encourage students to ask their questions of one another during the discussion. By posting a chart of the Question Starters in your room, you can stimulate students to ask thought-provoking questions during future discussions in your classroom—acknowledge and celebrate their smart thinking when they do!

Consider using Question Starters to help revamp the typical, but often useless, homework assignment of "Read Chapter 5 and answer the questions." Instead, you may suggest, "Read Chapter 5 and *create your own questions and answers using Bloom's Taxonomy.*" When generating questions by themselves, students are taking more responsibility for thinking on their own. In addition, they have to pay more attention to their reading. Ultimately, you want to challenge students to write complex questions at high levels of Bloom. At first, however, students should practice writing questions at all levels. In this way, they will learn to recognize and distinguish levels of questions. They will begin to understand that to think deeply about something, they must ask themselves questions at high levels of the taxonomy—questions that evoke complex thought.

As mentioned earlier, the questions students create could be used for a Bloom's Jeopardy game or they could be included on a class assessment. As always, we must first model many times the quality of work we expect. We can teach students to ask meaningful questions that engage higher levels of thinking by having them use the Question Starters in daily discussions and writing tasks—and providing regular feedback on their efforts. (See Chapter 6 to learn another excellent strategy for teaching students to generate their own questions called the ReQuest strategy.)

■ ASSESSMENTS IN BLOOM

Designed as alternative assessments, Assessments in Bloom are end-of-unit activities or projects that you design at three levels of complexity. The first level is the most concrete, providing students a task at the knowledge, comprehension, or application levels of Bloom's Taxonomy. The middle level targets objectives at the application or analysis levels. The highest level requires students to engage in activities and thought processes at the analysis, evaluation, and/or synthesis levels of the hierarchy.

There are many ways you can use these multilevel activities in a differ-

BLOOM QUESTION STARTERS

Answering knowledge questions helps us recall previously learned material, facts, terms, and basic concepts.

Knowledge Questions:

- ❍ Can you define/name/list/recall/select/identify/match/locate...?
- ❍ How many . . . ? Who was . . . ? What . . . ? Which . . . ? When did . . . ?
- ❍ What do you know about . . . ?

Answering comprehension questions helps us show our understanding of facts and ideas by describing, explaining, and stating main ideas.

Comprehension Questions:

- ❍ How can you explain/outline the steps . . . ?
- ❍ Can you describe/discuss/elaborate . . . ?
- ❍ Can you retell/paraphrase/restate . . . ?
- ❍ Can you summarize . . . ?
- ❍ What is the main idea? What is this mostly about?

Answering application questions helps us to solve problems by using our knowledge in new situations.

Application Questions:

- ❍ How would you use...?
- ❍ What examples can you find...?
- ❍ How would you organize ___ to show ___?
- ❍ What approach/technique would you use to . . . ?
- ❍ How could you illustrate/demonstrate/show . . . ?
- ❍ What is another use for . . . ?
- ❍ What are some examples of . . . ?
- ❍ What else could ___ have done?
- ❍ What do you think ___ would have done if ___?

Answering analysis questions helps us to examine and break information into parts, identify motives/causes, note relationships, and organize our ideas.

Analysis Questions:

- ❍ What are the parts/features/properties/characteristics/functions of. . . ?
- ❍ Why did . . . happen?
- ❍ What is the relationship between . . . and . . . ?
- ❍ Which is fact, opinion, or inference?
- ❍ What are the advantages/disadvantages/causes/effects of . . . ?
- ❍ How would you categorize/classify/group . . . ?
- ❍ How does . . . compare to . . . ?
- ❍ How would you organize these ideas?
- ❍ What steps are important in the process of . . . ?

Evaluation Questions:

Answering evaluation questions helps us to defend and justify our beliefs, to make informed judgments, and to draw conclusions.

- ❍ Do you agree/disagree with…?
- ❍ What is your opinion…?
- ❍ How would you justify/defend/rate/evaluate/judge the value of…?
- ❍ Would it be better if…?
- ❍ Why was it better/worse that…?
- ❍ How would you prioritize/rank…?
- ❍ What choice would you have made…?
- ❍ Which is the best/worst…?
- ❍ What solution do you favor and why?
- ❍ Which is the better bargain?
- ❍ Why is it important…?
- ❍ Do you think… is a good example of…? Why or why not?
- ❍ What can we tell about the author's attitude toward…?
- ❍ What viewpoints can you identify?

Synthesis Questions:

Answering synthesis questions helps us put information together in a new way, to illustrate something from a different point of view, or to propose an alternative solution to a problem.

- ❍ Can you propose an alternative…?
- ❍ Can you design/invent/compose/create/arrange…?
- ❍ What changes would you make to solve…?
- ❍ How would you improve…?
- ❍ What do you think would happen if…?
- ❍ Can you predict the outcome if…?
- ❍ Can you think of an original way …?
- ❍ What could be done to minimize/maximize…?
- ❍ Can you formulate a theory for…?
- ❍ How do you think … would feel/react/respond…?
- ❍ Can you develop a new use for…?
- ❍ What solutions can you suggest for…?
- ❍ What could another title for this be?

entiated classroom. You can choose to individually assign students tasks that are an appropriate challenge for them. (See Chapter 7 for a more in-depth look at tiering assignments.) Or you can allow students to choose one activity from each level, providing choice for everyone but making sure that all students climb the taxonomy. Some teachers in the upper grades like to give students a choice of tasks, tying a grade of A, B, or C to the three levels. They hope this will encourage all students to want to reach the highest level. Most teachers of younger students prefer, instead, to assign tasks to individuals, allowing everyone to achieve an A if he or she completes the task at that level of competency. See Figures 4.2, 4.3, and 4.4 for examples of Assessments in Bloom on the topics of electricity, Mexico, and biographies. Samples of student work on assessments for their electricity unit appear on page 85.

Figure 4.2

ASSESSMENTS IN BLOOM: ELECTRICITY

Red Task:

Knowledge/Comprehension/Application

❍ Draw and label a diagram of a complete circuit.

❍ Gather and label a collage of objects that are conductors and insulators.

Blue Task:

Application/Analysis

❍ Use a graphic organizer (Venn diagram/T-chart) to explain how a parallel circuit compares with a series circuit.

❍ Design a poster illustrating three electrical safety tips.

Yellow Task:

Analysis/Evaluation/Synthesis

❍ Describe and illustrate at least two ways the world would be different if electricity had not been discovered.

❍ Create a brochure advertising the benefits of a new product that uses electricity.

(Created by Luciana Fonseca, Rosemary Cappelle, and Nicole Bartone/Fourth-grade teachers)

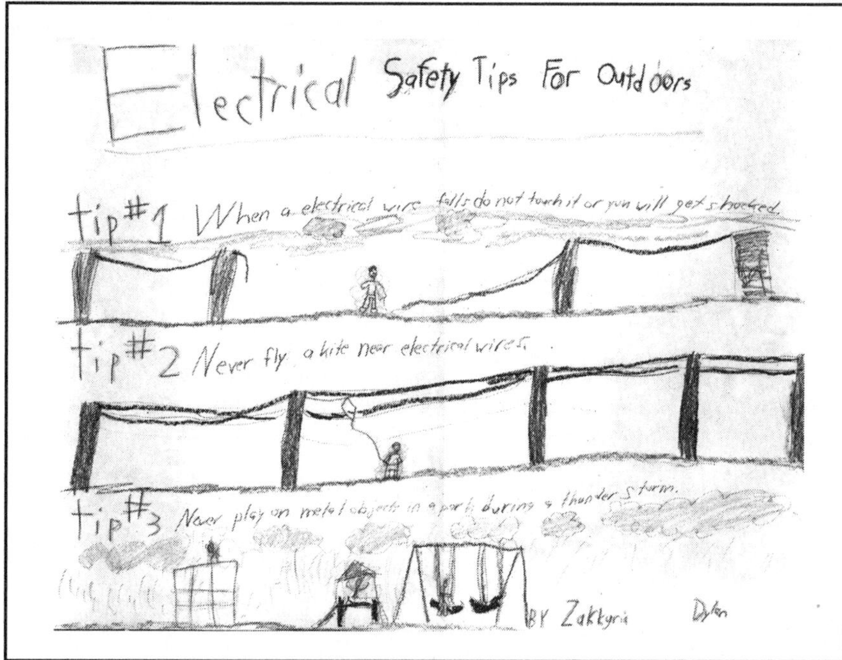

One pair of students designs a poster illustrating three electrical safety tips (application/analysis) [top] while another pair describes and illustrates two ways the world would be different if electricity had not been discovered (analysis/evaluation/synthesis) [bottom].

TEACHER REFLECTION

In our fourth-grade classes we chose an alternate assessment for our Electricity Unit: having students design a poster to show-what-you-know about electricity. Based on the students' reading levels, we assigned partners of same-readiness, and distributed a red, blue, or green task card to each group. The tasks were designed at three levels of Bloom's Taxonomy, and a choice of activities was provided at each level. The students needed to use their notebooks, science books, and experiment packets as resources for their posters.

The children really enjoyed working independently with one another and choosing the activity they preferred. We feel this activity worked extremely well because the final products [posters] all resembled one another even though the thinking and process skills required to complete each task were different. The children were working at an appropriate level of challenge for themselves, but they each benefited from the discussions, questions, and presentations of others working at different levels.

—DIANE BIANCANIELLO AND MARGE BUTTGEREIT/FOURTH-GRADE TEACHERS

Figure 4.3

ASSESSMENTS IN BLOOM: MEXICO

Red Task:

Knowledge/Comprehension/Application

❍ Create a map showing at least five major political and/or geographic features.

❍ Create a "Culture of Mexico" concept map (web) including terms related to: religion, holidays, music, food, population diversity, language.

Blue Task:

Application/Analysis

❍ In a visual format (poster, PowerPoint, diorama), show how where you live in Mexico (mountainous region, coastal area, urban or rural community) affects how you live (culture, job, chores, hobbies, etc.).

❍ Write a travel guide comparing the advantages and disadvantages of living in a mountainous or a coastal region.

Yellow Task:

Analysis/Evaluation/Synthesis

❍ Create an Artifact Box of items pertaining to Mexican history, government, geography, and culture.

❍ Compare the incomes, literacy rates, and mortality rates of Mexican and American citizens. Using this information, write a newspaper article describing how income, literacy rates, and mortality rates affect immigration trends in the United States today.

(Created by Martha Bergman, Janice Killelea, Peggie Nordmann/Fifth-grade teachers)

Figure 4.4

ASSESSMENTS IN BLOOM: FAMOUS PEOPLE/BIOGRAPHIES

Red Task:

Knowledge/Comprehension/Application

❍ Draw a timeline of important events in the person's life.

❍ List four reasons the person is famous (include photos/drawings)

Blue Task:

Application/Analysis

❍ Write an article for *People* magazine describing how the person's contributions affected society.

❍ Compare and contrast two famous people we have studied. Describe how they were similar/how they were different.

Yellow Task:

Analysis/Evaluation/Synthesis

❍ Describe and illustrate at least two ways the world would be different if this person had not existed.

❍ Choose the person you believe has contributed the most to society and write a recommendation for him or her to be entered into the Hall of Fame. Support your opinion with at least two reasons.

(Created by Merrick, NY, teachers)

Now that you've focused on increasing the complexity of your questions and the rigor of your assessments, it is time to take a look at how to make engaging, multiple intelligence–based activities more rigorous and complex. The key to deciding whether any activity is worth the time it takes to do is determining whether or not it will help students think critically. Chapter 5 shows you how to tie Gardner's multiple intelligences theory to Bloom's hierarchy of thinking for increased rigor in all your learning activities.

PRINCIPLES OF EFFECTIVE INSTRUCTION EXPLORED IN THIS CHAPTER:

Multiple pathways to learning

•

Respect for all types of learners

•

Reducing anxiety

•

Multiple intelligences/learning styles

•

Fostering intrinsic motivation

•

Choice

•

Lessons organized around the "big ideas"

CHAPTER 5

Making Multiple Intelligences Work

In the previous chapter, we focused on Bloom's Taxonomy and how to help students practice higher-order thinking. Now we are ready to explore how Bloom's hierarchy can impact learning when combined with Gardner's Multiple Intelligences theory. Many of us already use multiple intelligence–based activities in our classrooms. When assigning projects, for example, we allow students to choose from a variety of engaging formats that appeal to visual, kinesthetic, musical, and other intelligences. What we often don't hold students accountable for, however, is employing a high level of thinking while using a specific intelligence to show-what-they-know. The aim of this chapter is to provide strategies that help you keep the fun in classroom activities and still address a rigorous curriculum with state and national assessments.

Show Me the Research!

A few years ago I attended a workshop with Roger Taylor, who described the great success he had had with inner-city students attending his AP American History course. His course was organized around the principles of multiple intelligences, and his students had used their strengths and talents to master complex curriculum at the very highest levels of achievement. I clearly remember his comment that he believed "the best high school curriculum was a gutsy, content-driven curriculum taught with a middle school approach." A middle school teacher at the time, I smiled to myself and thought about all the experiential, interactive learning that was going on in our classrooms—and how we could not only better tailor it to students' aptitudes, but also deliver complex content.

Taylor had modeled his course on the work of Howard Gardner, professor of education at Harvard University and codirector of Project Zero, who challenged the traditional notion that intelligence was one inborn, fixed trait, easily measured by a paper-and-pencil test. By 1990, Gardner had identified at least eight intelligences that recognize different ways people are "smart," including

- *verbal-linguistic*
- *logical-mathematical*
- *spatial*
- *bodily-kinesthetic*
- *musical*
- *interpersonal*
- *intrapersonal*
- *naturalist* (1993)

Gardner has recently added a ninth intelligence, the *existential* intelligence, which he describes as the proclivity to pose and ponder questions about life, death, and ultimate realities.

Although they are not necessarily dependent on each other, these intelligences seldom operate in isolation. Every normal individual possesses varying degrees of each of these intelligences, but the ways in which intelligences combine and blend are as varied as the faces and the personalities of individuals.

HOWARD GARDNER

While many of us appreciate his identification of several intelligences and the choices they present for lesson planning, Howard Gardner cautions us against falling into a familiar trap of labeling students, this time using multiple intelligences. Instead, he suggests the importance of recognizing that students are an amalgam of all of the intelligences, interacting together, helping them to make meaning from the world (Nicholson-Nelson, 1998).

RELATED LITERATURE

Read Kristen Nicholson-Nelson's *Developing Students' Multiple Intelligences* (Scholastic, 1998) for many practical ideas that can help you integrate the theory of multiple intelligences into your instruction.

The enthusiasm that greeted Howard Gardner's work in educational circles when he first presented his findings on multiple intelligences was not shared by the psychological community. George A. Miller wrote in the *New York Times Book Review* in December 1983 that Gardner's "catalogue of intelligences is wrong" and "since nobody knows whether the educator should play to the student's strengths or bolster the student's weaknesses (or both), the new psychometrics does not seem to advance practical matters." E. D. Hirsch, in *The Schools We Need* (1996), argued that schools are not competent to classify and rank children on these "highly speculative psychological measures" and that the goals of a school should be developing students' competencies in the traditional curriculum: literacy, numeracy, and general knowledge. Once those common goals are agreed upon, he added, psychological classifications would seem to have "little function beyond the encouragement of respect and egalitarianism."

In a paper he presented at the American Educational Research Association in 2003, Gardner reveals that he never expected such an overwhelming response to his theory from the educational community. He maintains that he is a psychologist, not an educator, and that he does not presume to know how to teach a class of young students. His interest, he maintains, lies in trying to understand the organization of human abilities in the brain.

People who lean on logic and philosophy and rational exposition end by starving the best part of the mind.
WILLIAM BUTLER YEATS

Still, educators continue to cite his theory in support of a different kind of teaching, one that recognizes a different kind of intelligence. Among educators today who continue to praise his work is Thomas Armstrong, award-winning author and speaker on issues related to learning and human development. He believes that teachers should be trained to present their lessons in a wide variety of ways, using music, cooperative learning, art, role play, multimedia, inner reflection, and much more (1998, 2000). By addressing multiple intelligences, he suggests, we can reach many more of our learners.

In "Variations on a Theme: How Teachers Interpret MI Theory" (1997), Linda Campbell describes five approaches to curriculum change that schools, informed by Gardner's theory, are making:

- Lesson design (team-teaching and teachers focusing on their own intelligence strength; using all or several of the intelligences in lessons; asking students their opinions on how best to learn)
- Interdisciplinary units
- Student projects
- Assessments (that allow students to show-what-they-know in their preferred way while meeting the teacher's criteria for quality)
- Apprenticeships (that allow students to gain mastery over a valued skill gradually, with effort and discipline over time)

(You will be able to use the information in this chapter to address the first four of these approaches in your own classroom.)

David Lazear, an author, trainer, and authority on the practical application of multiple intelligences in business and education, believes we have been given inaccurate and misleading information about intelligence and what makes us smart. In his book *OutSmart Yourself* (2004), he suggests that our IQ measures a small range of our human intellectual capacities, and that, in fact, we are smart in a number of ways. His Eight Kinds of Smart are labeled in a language that even our primary learners can understand. They include: ImageSmart (spatial intelligence), LogicSmart (logical-mathematical intelligence), WordSmart (verbal-linguistic intelligence), BodySmart (bodily-kinesthetic intelligence), SoundSmart (musical intelligence), NatureSmart (naturalist intelligence), PeopleSmart (interpersonal intelligence), and SelfSmart (intrapersonal intelligence). He argues that we are born with all these intelligences and that once we awaken them within ourselves, we will think, work, and learn smarter.

So, what does all this mean for our classrooms? Does it matter whether or not we address multiple intelligences in our classes? How can we apply multiple intelligences theory and still have time for our entire curriculum with all its content?

When I give my students options during a learning activity to use one of several multiple intelligences, I can feel palpable enthusiasm in my classroom. The attention, interest, and motivation generated by addressing their preferences lead to teaching and learning that becomes so much more meaningful and long-lasting. I can't imagine not using multiple intelligences, even if there continues to be controversy over their use. The reason I embrace MI is the zeal it evokes in my students.

—MIDDLE-SCHOOL TEACHER

Putting Research Into Action

When I talk to my own children about memories of meaningful experiences they had when they were in school, they report vivid recollections of certain classroom activities. Their fondest memories include a time capsule of gathered artifacts buried in fifth grade and opened upon graduation from high school; a newscast performed in costume to demonstrate what they understood about life in the Colonial period; a group project preparing Egyptian mummies and tombs; a four-season fashion show performed with props in their foreign language classroom; a PowerPoint presentation (accompanied by theme music from the *Rocky* soundtrack) designed and delivered in health class to convince peers about the need to maintain a healthy lifestyle; and the construction of a rotating fork made of battery-powered Legos to spin spaghetti, an invention that met a perceived need. As you can see, my sons preferred interpersonal, bodily-kinesthetic, musical, and logical-mathematical activities to the more traditional verbal-linguistic activities of most classrooms. Clearly, for them the most meaningful school activities were ones that incorporated several intelligences working together to help them improve their understanding of the world around them.

Now don't get me wrong. The line in the sand has been drawn regarding the measure of student success in most states. And to that end, all students need to be able to do well on the verbal-linguistic and logical-mathematical components of the state assessments. But to ignore the power that the other intelligences play in motivating students in school is to miss the point. To be certain, Gardner has had his detractors, but there are hundreds of schools in this country that are organized primarily around learning

KEY IDEA

By "hooking" students through their strengths and talents, we invite them to stick with us when writing, math, or history gets too difficult for them in school.

through multiple intelligences and that report great success on local as well as state assessments. When students are intrinsically motivated to learn, as they are when provided with choice and the ability to use their strengths and talents in the classroom, their learning is much greater. When our students are encouraged to reach their fullest potential through individual dispositions and preferences, the likelihood of their success on assessments increases.

Unfortunately, teachers have often been taught that multiple intelligence–based activities are "fun," "extra" activities requiring little, if any, critical thinking to complete. Although most teachers appreciate products, projects, and presentations that are multiple intelligence–based, many now refuse to assign activities that seem to offer little educational value, even if they are motivating and engaging. I would argue that they have thrown the baby out with the bathwater.

To make these activities worthy of the time spent in class sharing the products and equal to the rigor required of the assessments, we must link multiple intelligence–based activities to higher levels of thinking, a guiding principle I call "Gardner in Bloom." It *is* possible to create complex and rigorous learning opportunities that link the curriculum, standards, and assessment with multiple intelligences—and in doing so, invite students to be fully engaged in personally appealing, sense-making activities that require higher-order thinking. The more we create such opportunities for our students, the more likely they will eagerly engage in and benefit from the learning experiences we provide.

RELATED LITERATURE

Diane Heacox's Integration Matrix is another tool for designing activities with multiple challenge levels, as well as multiple intelligences. Read her book *Differentiating Instruction in the Regular Classroom* (Free Spirit Publishing, 2002).

Strategies

The strategies that follow show you how to integrate multiple intelligence–based activities as you design your curriculum and simultaneously create rigorous tasks that challenge each student appropriately. The How I Am Smart checklist (page 94) gives students a way to assess their own strengths and preferences with regards to multiple intelligences. The Multiple Intelligence–Based Product List (Figure 5.1 on page 95) provides you with a variety of activities from which to choose when designing alternative assessments that appeal to students' unique talents and interests. Planning With Gardner in Bloom (Figure 5.2, page 96) offers helpful examples of multiple intelligence–based activities that are both engaging and complex. Finally, the Gardner in Bloom practice worksheet and planning template (pages 98 and 101) provide you with practice designing your own activities that stimulate critical thinking. You'll also find examples of Gardner in Bloom activities that are both assessment-driven and fun to do.

■ HOW I AM SMART CHECKLIST

Use the How I Am Smart checklist on page 94 to help students assess their strengths at the beginning of the year. Provide students with a copy of the checklist and ask them to check any of the statements that apply to themselves. Have students share their intelligence strengths (any intelligence for which they've checked four or more statements) with the rest of the class and create a class graph or chart to show the different ways students are all smart. Tell students that from time to time you will be offering them choices of activities and that it will be interesting to see whether they choose activities that are related to their preferences and how well they learn from and enjoy the activities.

Don't be surprised if some children tend to choose the same type of activity again and again. Keep in mind Gardner's own caveat not to label students by identified strengths but instead to recognize these strengths as preferences and to encourage students to try activities in other categories from time to time as well. Younger children in particular should be encouraged to try different types of activities because they haven't had time to develop all of their aptitudes. Students will make sense of the world as they process information using several intelligences at once.

Hold students accountable for using critical-thinking skills when using one of Gardner's multiple intelligence–based activities.

■ MULTIPLE INTELLIGENCE–BASED PRODUCTS

Figure 5.1 provides a list of open-ended multiple intelligence–based products that students may find engaging. Use this list as you create homework options or end-of-unit projects that appeal to a range of students. It will remind you to vary the activities among the eight intelligences. Some teachers give this list to eager students who want to earn extra credit. These students choose from among the different options to show-what-they-know about a topic they have been studying.

■ PLANNING WITH GARDNER IN BLOOM

In Figure 5.2 I have created ten examples to illustrate how teachers might choose multiple intelligence–based products and then make them more rigorous. The figure shows, for example, the difference between a very open-ended activity, such as "Write three journal entries in an Irish immigrant's diary," and one that asks students to use specific critical thinking skills, such as "Write three journal entries in an Irish immigrant's diary *that compare three ways* life in Ireland was different from the life found in New York City."

LEARNING
SELF-ASSESSMENT
ACTIVITY

HOW I AM SMART

Put a check next to any of the statements that apply to you.

Verbal-Linguistic Intelligence

___ I like to read, write, use words.
___ I enjoy puzzles, word games, rhymes, etc.
___ Spelling is easy for me.
___ My vocabulary is strong.
___ I like to do research about topics I'm interested in.
___ I enjoy stories and storytelling.

Logical-Mathematical Intelligence

___ I enjoy numbers, math, and computers.
___ I like strategy games like chess.
___ I like to analyze and solve problems.
___ I like organization, structure, and logical sequences.
___ I enjoy charts, graphs, statistics, data.
___ I like designing and conducting experiments.

Spatial Intelligence

___ I enjoy drawing, doodling.
___ I like color.
___ I like videos, movies, and books with diagrams and photographs.
___ I can close my eyes and "picture in my mind."
___ I can find my way in new places.
___ I enjoy using maps, blueprints, spreadsheets, graphic organizers.

Bodily-Kinesthetic Intelligence

___ I like to move around; I can't sit still for long.
___ I enjoy doing, not watching.
___ I like to use my hands.
___ I am very coordinated.
___ I enjoy sports and activities.
___ I like to make/build/construct things.

Musical Intelligence

___ I enjoy music.
___ I have a good sense of rhythm.
___ I remember melodies and songs.
___ I play an instrument.
___ I sing.
___ I'm sensitive to noise and sounds.

Interpersonal Intelligence

___ I like to be with people.
___ I'm a good leader.
___ I like working in groups.
___ I have a lot of friends.
___ I don't like working alone.
___ I understand how other people feel in situations.

Intrapersonal Intelligence

___ I set goals for myself.
___ I like to work alone.
___ I know a lot about myself.
___ I have a strong sense of fairness.
___ I am an individual with my own ideas.
___ I have my own personal hobbies.

Naturalist Intelligence

___ I enjoy being in the outdoors.
___ I observe and see patterns.
___ I am sensitive to nature.
___ I enjoy taking care of animals and plants.
___ I appreciate the environment.
___ I like to group and classify things around me.

Figure 5.1

A Multiple Intelligence–Based Product List

Verbal-Linguistic:

- ❍ Write a book, poem, myth, or news article about…
- ❍ Design a checklist for…
- ❍ Research a topic and take notes…
- ❍ Write a travel brochure/newsletter…
- ❍ Create a set of newspaper headlines…
- ❍ Use storytelling to explain…

Logical-Mathematical:

- ❍ Conduct a survey, graph your results, and draw conclusions...
- ❍ Construct a visual timeline…
- ❍ Design and conduct an experiment to prove…
- ❍ Create or play a dice game and record…
- ❍ Complete a graphic organizer…
- ❍ Create a word problem based on _______ …

Bodily-Kinesthetic:

- ❍ Bring hands-on materials to demonstrate…
- ❍ Make a videotape of…
- ❍ Create a museum exhibit to show…
- ❍ Create a play, role-play, or use props…
- ❍ Gather a Treasure Chest/Artifact Box to show…
- ❍ Create a movement or sequence of movements to explain…

Intrapersonal:

- ❍ Keep a diary about…
- ❍ Reflect on your own learning process…
- ❍ Write an advice column…
- ❍ Record in a progress chart your accomplishments toward a goal…
- ❍ Create an All About Me Scrapbook (about a character, historical figure, inventor, etc.)…
- ❍ Complete a Venn diagram that compares you and a character or historical figure…

Spatial:

- ❍ Design a greeting card or postcard…
- ❍ Create a PhotoJournal about…
- ❍ Create a game that teaches the concept of…
- ❍ Create a scrapbook…
- ❍ Find examples of fine art, architecture, or sculpture to symbolize the story/reflect the time period…
- ❍ Take photographs/Use photographs to…

Musical:

- ❍ Interpret a song from a specific time period…
- ❍ Gather examples of music that reflect the mood of a book or a time period…
- ❍ Analyze different types of poems for their patterns of rhyme, rhythm, or sounds
- ❍ Play a piece of music to illustrate…
- ❍ Make an instrument and use it to demonstrate…

Naturalist:

- ❍ Write a PhotoJournal about…
- ❍ Take a virtual field trip via the Internet to…
- ❍ Write and illustrate a postcard from…
- ❍ Gather or plan a collection of objects that…
- ❍ E-mail keypals in other places to learn…
- ❍ Use binoculars, microscopes, magnifiers, or telescopes to…

Interpersonal:

- ❍ Evaluate your group's performance…
- ❍ Present a news show/host a talk show…
- ❍ Interview several people about…
- ❍ Lead a group discussion on…
- ❍ Teach the class about…
- ❍ Conduct a group or class meeting to discuss…

Figure 5.2

PLANNING WITH GARDNER IN BLOOM

Examples of Multiple Intelligence–Based Activities at Higher Levels of Complexity

Multiple Intelligence–Based Activity	**How It Addresses Critical Thinking** (Analysis, Synthesis, Evaluation)
Social Studies: (*Intrapersonal*) Write three journal entries in an Irish immigrant's diary...	that compare three ways life in Ireland was different from the life found in New York City. (*Analysis*)
Social Studies: (*Verbal-Linguistic*) Write three headlines that you would find in the *Renaissance Times*...	that show your understanding of how life has changed since the Middle Ages. (*Analysis*)
Math: (*Verbal-Linguistic*) Write a book for children...	that explains and compares rational numbers and irrational numbers. (*Analysis/Synthesis*)
Math: (*Bodily-Kinesthetic*) Gather an Artifact Box that includes at least ten items in your everyday life...	that use or represent fractions (decimals, percents, measurement, geometric shapes, etc.). *(Application)*
LOTE (Languages Other Than English): (*Spatial/Logical-Mathematical*) Create a visual timeline of your life with at least five events and five captions...	that shows your understanding of the difference between the preterite and imperfect tenses. (*Analysis*)
LOTE (Languages Other Than English): (*Interpersonal*) Present a meteorologist's report...	describing one day's season, weather, suggested clothing, and possible activities. (*Analysis*)
English: (*Verbal-Linguistic*) Invent your own mythological character to invite to dinner...	and create a story about the events of dinner based on the personality of your character. (*Synthesis*)
English: (*Bodily-Kinesthetic*) Create a Treasure Chest for the chapter book/novel we are reading...	that demonstrates your understanding of the setting, the characters, the symbols, and the themes. Include an explanation of each item you include. (*Analysis*)
Science: (*Verbal-Linguistic/Spatial*) Create an illustrated booklet on the body systems...	to show how at least two organs function in more than one system. (*Analysis/Synthesis*)
Science: (*Naturalist/Spatial*) Create a PhotoJournal about the biome we are studying...	that compares plant life, animal life, land, and climate in the winter and the summer. (*Synthesis*)

■ GARDNER IN BLOOM PRACTICE WORKSHEET

The Gardner in Bloom Practice Worksheet on page 98 gives you experience in developing appropriately challenging multiple intelligence–based activities. I have suggested multiple intelligence–based activities in the left column. You may adapt the idea to a specific curriculum-based activity that addresses critical thinking at the analysis, synthesis, or evaluation levels of Bloom's Taxonomy in the right column. These activities should require students to analyze information, note relationships and changes over time, sequence events, recognize similarities and distinguish differences, illustrate opposing points of view, create new ideas, and support opinions with evidence. As you develop homework options or alternative assessments for each new unit, keep this two-column structure in mind to help you create activities that are both engaging and rigorous.

■ GARDNER IN BLOOM ACTIVITIES

Once you are comfortable with linking multiple intelligence–based activities to higher-level thinking skills, you can design end-of-unit projects and/or alternative assessments that integrate the best of Gardner and Bloom while still addressing curriculum standards and state assessments.

Figures 5.3 and 5.4 illustrate how a foreign language teacher and an English language arts teacher offer end-of-unit project choices to their students and still address their standards and assessments. You will notice that although both teachers provide four choices of activities, each choice addresses several of the same key understandings, skills, or focus questions identified as important to the unit. The teachers have made clear what *all students* must know and be able to do. The choice is in the option of *how* to show-what-you-know. To design worthwhile Gardner in Bloom activities, you must keep several things in mind. First, decide on two to four key understandings that all students must demonstrate through their choice of activity. Next, choose four different multiple intelligence–based activities to offer variety to students. Finally, design the four activities, making sure that each addresses the key understandings at high levels of critical thinking. (See "Things to Consider: Gardner in Bloom Activities.") The planning template on page 101 will remind you to label each activity with the multiple intelligence and the appropriate level of Bloom's Taxonomy. Provide the four Gardner in Bloom choices to students at the beginning or midway through your unit and allow them to choose one activity as an alternative assessment to a pen-and-pencil exam.

You can use the reproducible rubric on page 102 to help you assess the Gardner in Bloom activities or you can design one with students. The rubric included here is generic enough to work with written reports, as well as orally or visually presented projects.

Gardner in Bloom activities tie multiple intelligence–based activities to rigorous thinking.

Designing Multiple Intelligence–Based Activities at Higher Levels of Complexity

As you develop a list of instructional activities, use this worksheet to help check that the activities target one or more of the intelligences and, more importantly, meet critical-thinking goals.

Add a curriculum focus for each multiple intelligence–based activity in the left column, and in the right column add specific instructions that guide students to complete each activity at a high level of complexity. You'll find a Bloom's Taxonomy chart on page 80 for reference.

Choose a Multiple Intelligence–Based Activity **(MI)**	**How Does It Address Critical Thinking at Higher Levels of Complexity?** (Bloom's Taxonomy) **Levels:** Analysis, Synthesis, Evaluation
EXAMPLE: **Gather an Artifact Box...** with some items representing the 1920s **MI:** Bodily-Kinesthetic	**that examines...** the social, cultural, and technological aspects of this decade. **Level:** Analysis
Write a children's book... **MI:** Verbal-Linguistic	**that distinguishes different kinds of...** **Level:**
Create a PhotoJournal... **MI:** Spatial	**that compares and contrasts...** **Level:**
Conduct a survey and graph results... **MI:** Interpersonal/Logical-Mathematical	**that draw conclusions about...** **Level:**
Create two headlines... **MI:** Verbal-Linguistic	**that show opposing viewpoints about...** **Level:**
Create an All About Me Scrapbook... **MI:** Intrapersonal	**that sequences the life of...** **Level:**

Figure 5.3

GARDNER IN BLOOM ACTIVITIES

Topic: CHARACTERIZATION (Language Arts—Grade 6)

Key Understandings/Skills/Focus Questions:

- How does a character change over time?
- How does an author develop an understanding of the character?
- How do decisions and events in a story impact a character's life?

Create a chart to show what you've learned about the main character. Include clues from the author about 1) how the character looks; 2) what the character does; 3) what the character says, thinks, or feels; and 4) how other characters respond to him/her. Include at least two clues for each aspect of character. **Bloom:** Analysis **MI:** Logical-Mathematical	**Create a visual timeline** of your main character that illustrates and briefly describes important decisions the character makes and how he/she changes from the beginning to the end of the story. **Bloom:** Analysis **MI:** Spatial
Compose your own short story about a character. Be sure to develop your character by describing his/her looks, explaining what he/she does, sharing what he/she says, thinks, or feels. Ask yourself: How do other characters respond to my character? How does he or she change? What happens that might change him or her? **Bloom:** Analysis **MI:** Verbal-Linguistic	**Gather a Treasure Chest** (items, pictures, quotes, maps, symbols, sketches, etc.) that reflect your character's traits, conflicts, and ways he/she overcame obstacles in life. Include a brief written description of the significance of each item. **Bloom:** Analysis **MI:** Bodily-Kinesthetic

Adapted from a workshop with Wantagh teachers

Figure 5.4

GARDNER IN BLOOM ACTIVITIES

Topic: CLOTHING (Foreign Language—Grade 8)

Key Understandings/Skills/Focus Questions:

- Identify articles of clothing and accessories.
- Use correct forms of *adjectives* and *colors* to describe seasonal clothing (refer to *size*, as well*)*
- Use color, size, and price descriptions to select appropriate clothing

Write four cards to be read at a fashion show. Describe the outfits to be worn by four models, each representing one of the seasons. (*Include adjectives, color, price.*) **Bloom:** Analysis **MI:** Verbal-Linguistic	**Create a brochure** for traveling to different tourist attractions in a foreign country. Highlight four different types of activities and the appropriate dress for each. Describe at least four outfits, using adjectives and color. **Bloom:** Synthesis **MI:** Spatial/Logical-Mathematical
Present a four-season fashion show to your classmates using a bag of clothing props. Use complete sentences. (*Include adjectives, color, price.*) **Bloom:** Analysis **MI:** Bodily-Kinesthetic	**Write and present a dialogue** of at least ten exchanges about shopping for clothing and/or accessories. In your conversation, discuss color, size, and price, and use adjectives to describe at least two pieces of clothing. **Bloom:** Synthesis **MI:** Interpersonal

Adapted from a workshop with Wantagh teachers

GARDNER IN BLOOM

Topic/Concept: ______________________________

Key Understandings/Skills/Focus Questions:

- ______________________________
- ______________________________
- ______________________________

Bloom: **MI:**	**Bloom:** **MI:**
Bloom: **MI:**	**Bloom:** **MI:**

RUBRIC

Name of student: ______________________________

Project: ______________________________

Criteria:	**Points earned:** 4	3	2	1
I have fulfilled all the requirements of this project.				
My project is accurate and it contains several details to support my main ideas.				
My presentation is visually neat or clearly communicated.				
My project shows effort and creativity.				
My project is on time.				

Total points I have earned: __________

Multiplied by 5 = __________ %

Things to Consider: Gardner in Bloom Activities

When designing Gardner in Bloom activities have I

❍ chosen a variety of multiple intelligence–based activities to appeal to the strengths, talents, and interests of my diverse students?

❍ made sure that the thinking elicited by each of the tasks is rigorous enough to challenge specific groups or individuals in my class?

❍ selected activities that require students to analyze, compare and contrast, sort and classify, consider different perspectives, judge an event or outcome, determine the importance or value of something, suggest an alternative solution, note changes over time, develop metaphors, or create an original scenario?

By relating multiple intelligences to critical thinking and providing choice for students from among exciting options, you are opening up multiple pathways for students to learn. Showing respect for all types of learners in this way reduces the anxiety of struggling learners and extends opportunities for advanced learners, as well. If you keep your eye on the big ideas and focus primarily on higher-order thinking, there is no reason to eliminate fun from your classroom because of new assessments. In fact, students may never be more prepared for the assessments than they are in an environment that recognizes their uniqueness and honors it—and therefore, makes learning more accessible for them.

Now that we've explored differentiation by student strengths and complexity, we can move on to differentiation by lesson design. Chapter 6 helps you deliver effective instruction through flexible groupings.

PRINCIPLES OF EFFECTIVE INSTRUCTION EXPLORED IN THIS CHAPTER:

Multiple pathways to learning

•

Ongoing and frequent assessments

•

Respect for all types of learners

•

Multiple Intelligences/learning styles

•

Varying teaching styles

•

Constructivist practices

•

A student-centered classroom

•

Flexible groupings

CHAPTER 6

Maximizing Student Learning With Flexible Groupings

It's easy for some students to get lost in large-group discussions. But those quiet, shy students, who rarely participate in whole-class exchanges, often become more involved when they work with a partner. On the other hand, those students who tend to dominate class discussions must step back and take their lead from other students when they participate in a cooperative group activity. Students not only learn academic content and important skills from their peers in group settings, they learn how to be productive group members in a variety of situations. This chapter explores ways to maximize student learning and to encourage the participation of all types of learners by varying our grouping strategies and choosing appropriate teaching methods for different types of groups.

Show Me the Research!

Flexible instructional grouping is the thoughtful and deliberate match between students and their specific needs. Although many teachers use small groups in their classrooms, a differentiated classroom is marked by a flow of whole-class, small-group, and individual opportunities to acquire and use information in new ways. In a differentiated classroom, a teacher uses a variety of strategies for grouping students based on their level of readiness (skill-level or background knowledge) or interest. Each decision for grouping is based on making the appropriate match between the task and the student.

The flexible use of student groups is the heart of a differentiated classroom. (HEACOX, 2002).

When experienced teachers plan, their grouping choices are informed by their answer to the question, "Is this task designed to tap into a student strength or is it designed to strengthen a weakness?" If the answer is to tap into a student strength, we usually opt for a *mixed-ability, interest-based group* that contains students of different academic strengths and experiences who share a common interest in a topic or type of activity. If the answer is to strengthen a student weakness, we usually organize a *homogeneous, same-ability group*, in which we group students by academic need. D. Ray Reutzel, a professor of education at Brigham Young University, explains that same-ability groups are "periodically created, modified, or disbanded to meet new needs as they arise." Another use for this format is to extend students' understanding, as Reutzel puts it, to "teach a temporary group of students a particular procedure, literary stylistic device, skill, or strategy they have yet to learn and apply" (1999). This "needs grouping" allows us to focus our teaching effectively on students who require the same level of support or challenge. The way to determine which students have similar needs and should be grouped together is through careful and frequent assessment and observation.

In flexible group settings, both the struggling learner and the advanced learner enjoy opportunities for success. Students who need modifications benefit from cooperative experiences that promote social interaction. Strategically formed groups can be flexibly arranged so that struggling students are placed in a situation in which they can exhibit their strengths (Wrubel, 2002). Too often, however, we focus only on the struggling learners and providing the appropriate setting for them. We must not forget that advanced learners' needs must be addressed as well. Placing them in groups with students of similar abilities, interests, and/or learning styles will accommodate some of their needs and allow them to work in more independent, abstract, and divergent ways than is typically possible in other group settings.

It's important not to forget the needs of advanced learners in our mixed-readiness classrooms. From time to time, place them in groups with students of similar abilities and allow them to work together in more independent, abstract, and divergent ways.

Students need varying amounts of direction and structure to learn and perform well in group settings (Heacox, 2002). For this reason, it is extremely important to provide and frequently review student guidelines for performance in groups. Part of the group task should be an evaluation of how students function both individually and as a group. With your entire class, you can brainstorm a few behaviors that will maximize the effectiveness of working in groups, such as cooperating with others, listening actively to other group members, participating, and staying on task, sharing responsibility, and helping others. After the task is over, ask students to evaluate themselves and their peers on their performance.

Caldwell and Ford (2002) cite a variety of benefits for using flexible groupings over the more predominant method of whole-class instruction. Among these benefits, students learn to:

- act more independently and set personal goals.
- absorb content while acquiring interpersonal and cooperative skills.
- be accountable to others when part of a group.
- work with a noise level that does not detract from the work of others.
- move around the room without causing disruption.

Positive relationships form among students who work in a variety of groupings, rather than in just one grouping format. Cliques are less likely to form. Students get to see their peers' strengths, not only their weaknesses, and this engenders respect for one another. Finding themselves in working situations where they need to cooperate and learn from different people, these students are more likely to be able to work with others outside the classroom. In general, flexible groups offer an exciting alternative to whole-class work and provide a structure that allows for more creativity on the part of the teacher.

Once we understand how to use flexible groupings, we can choose from a wide array of instructional strategies that meet our curriculum demands and utilize flexible groupings. Forsten, Grant, and Hollas (2002) explain that when we differentiate instruction, it is important to use "instructional intelligence," the ability to choose wisely from the variety of methods and strategies we have gathered—knowing when and with whom to use them.

If the only tool you have is a hammer, you will tend to see every problem as a nail.
ABRAHAM MASLOW

According to Silver, Strong, and Perini, "A repertoire of effective teaching strategies is one of the teacher's best means of reaching the full range of learners in the classroom and of making learning deep and memorable for students" (2000). By rotating strategies and using flexible groupings throughout the course of a unit, we can be sure to accommodate students' dominant learning styles, as well as challenge them to work in their less preferred styles (Strong, Perini, and Silver, 2004). When we organize for instruction, we need to consider the unique needs, desires, strengths, interests, preferences, and learning styles of our diverse students. No one way will work for all students. Strategically mixing methods and strategies will make our lessons more accessible and our students more enthusiastic. Abraham Maslow said, "If the only tool you have is a hammer, you will tend to see every problem as a nail." We must expand our comfortable instructional-delivery systems to include new tools that meet the needs of more of our students.

Putting Research Into Action

Early on in my teaching, I struggled to keep the attention of my students for an entire class period. I was young and full of energy, so at the time, zipping around the room and actively dramatizing my lessons seemed like a reasonable way to gain and keep their attention. After a while, however, I noticed that even this flurry of activity could not sustain the focus of many of my students. Some needed more guidance, repeated modeling, and more quiet time for reflection; others, those who had caught on quickly, were frustrated by a slower pace of instruction than they required and few opportunities to creatively work on their own. Some were shy and hesitant to speak in front of the whole class; others tried to dominate the discussions during each day's lessons. I realized that I needed to include different types of groupings and techniques that engaged learners while respecting their individual differences.

I began to try some grouping strategies my colleagues were using successfully. I experimented first with the smallest grouping, pairs. As I became comfortable with one type of grouping, I tried out a new format.

If students aren't learning the way that we teach, then we need to teach them in the way that they learn.
CAROL ANN TOMLINSON

■ STUDY BUDDIES/LEARNING PARTNERS

Taking a step away from my usual whole-class grouping, I first introduced my class to Study Buddies or Learning Partners. (The name you and your students choose will depend on their grade-level and maturity—younger students tend to prefer Study Buddies while older students tend to prefer Learning Partners.) Pairing students offered a safe learning structure in which partners could share their understandings and articulate what they were coming to know. This grouping also offered each student much more "on" time for active learning than a whole-group setting did. Through regular discussions in which partners were required to use content-specific vocabulary, their comprehension increased. Partners were able to perform "accuracy checks" on each other's work, providing additional feedback to one another at times when I could not reach each student. I watched students learn how to learn from each other as they discussed their personal strategies for studying the content.

My fear of not being able to bring students back from a five-minute pairing activity diminished as my students gained experience working in pairs. As partnering activities became more routine, students required less transition time to move from the whole group to pairs and back again. If you have never used Study Buddies or Learning Partners before, one strategy I recommend is to have students practice moving from large group into partners and back again before you actually assign a task for them to complete. Treat it like a game, and time students to see if they can reduce the number of seconds it takes to make the transition.

TEACHER REFLECTION

Splitting my class randomly in half and working with one group while the other group completes an assigned task allows me to more easily assess my students' needs. My students enjoy the smaller groupings and the novelty of the format. They've even learned to stay on task during their ten-minute independent time.

—SIXTH-GRADE TEACHER

■ HALF-CLASS/HALF-CLASS

After my Study Buddies were working well, I divided my class into two random groups. My goal was twofold: to be able to work with fewer students at one time and to help students (*and myself*) become comfortable with different activities going on at the same time in the room. First, I would make sure that all students understood the learning goals and behavior expectations for the independent task. Then, I would work for ten minutes with one group, while the second group would read, create graphic organizers, or write a reflection about something they had learned from a previous lesson. Then, I would have the groups switch. This Half-Class/Half-Class grouping allowed me to assess my students more easily because I was working with fewer at one time.

When you first try this grouping, you can expect that some students in the group working independently will not begin the task quickly enough, others will not stay on task, and still others will be distracted by the discussion you are having with the other half of the students. Don't give up on the strategy; instead, use it even more frequently. Once your students get used to the routine and begin to realize that there is only a brief time period in which to complete the assigned task, they will begin to get to work more quickly. Allow them to use their Study Buddies for brief consultations when they are uncertain about what to do. Most students will become less distracted with having more than one thing going on in their environment. At the end of your Half-Class/Half-Class grouping, bring the whole class together to share, and hold each student accountable for his own independent written work. You will find that most students in your class will like the novelty of the groupings, the change of pace it provides, and the freedom to work quietly with a partner, if needed.

■ SMALL-GROUP INSTRUCTION

As I gained confidence in my ability to manage more than one group at a time, I began to add small-group instruction to my repertoire. Small groups, in contrast to the half-class model, offered more opportunities for me to differentiate instruction—to respond appropriately to cognitive differences among my students as well as to their varied learning interests.

I quickly discovered that using small groups of mixed-ability students every time we engaged in group work did not address the varied needs, interests, and learning styles of my students. I began to plan needs groupings based on a specific skill that several students were having difficulty with. For five to ten minutes I would work with that same-readiness group, while the rest of the class engaged in independent or paired practice.

I've used this technique quite successfully in foreign language classes: I would call together a small group of Spanish I students to coach them through answering oral questions about their family. Meanwhile, the rest of the class (those already proficient at answering the basic questions) would work in pairs to create a dialogue in which they introduce their family members to a classmate. At other times, I have formed several small, mixed-readiness groups around similar interests for research. In that same class, I occasionally placed students in groups organized by high-interest topics such as Mexican food, holidays, and bullfighting. Alternatively, I've had students form their own groups around their learning preferences in which they created projects based on multiple intelligences. One year, a unit on weather and clothing produced a four-season fashion show, a catalog of seasonal outfits, and an interview in Spanish with a travel agent about what to wear while traveling during different seasons in Spain. I have also used mixed-readiness groups in Jigsaw activities (pages 117–120), in which each group member became an expert on a particular area of the group's study focus and then taught the whole group about what they had learned.

■ FLEXIBLE GROUPING IN YOUR CLASSROOM

Keep in mind that we all tend to seek methods and set up classroom structures that appeal to *our own* learning preferences. If you are uncomfortable with group work, you'll likely avoid using groups, even though there is much research to support their use. I encourage teachers unfamiliar with cooperative grouping strategies to read the works of Spencer Kagan or David and Roger Johnson and Edith Johnson Holubec (see Related Literature below), to visit the classrooms of and talk to teachers who are using groups effectively, and to start with brief, small exercises in cooperative grouping. Many teachers have successfully begun to use small groups after beginning with the Half-Class/Half-Class strategy I described above.

RELATED LITERATURE

Read the following books to learn more about how to form effective cooperative groups:

Spencer Kagan's *Cooperative Learning* (Allyn and Bacon, 1994).

David Johnson, Roger Johnson, and Edith Johnson Holubec's *Circles of Learning: Cooperation in the Classroom* (Interaction Book Co., 1993).

David Johnson, Roger Johnson, and Edith Johnson Holubec's *Advanced Cooperative Learning* (Interaction Book Co., 1998).

As you integrate flexible, shifting group formats into your teaching routine, you'll need to consider a variety of teaching methods that support diverse learners in each format. How will students share responsibility for their work? Will they take on different roles? Will there be a teacher-led component? Would it help to move from small to large group for closure or vice versa? These are the types of questions that teachers address when differentiating instruction in groups. It takes a broad repertoire of approaches to maximize student learning in our classroom. By providing alternative ways of understanding, including right- and left-brain activities, by varying learning styles and degrees of learner independence, and by mixing groupings, methodologies and teaching strategies, you ensure that students actively participate in their own learning. You'll find a selection of strategies to use with groups of different sizes in the next section.

Strategies

Using flexible grouping to help us differentiate our instructional strategies, we can choose from a variety of strategies that address the learner as an individual, a partner, a member of a small group, and a part of a larger class community. When we select activities for the learner *as an individual*, we help our students develop metacognitive skills and grow in independence. My Learning Log and My Opinions Journal are two useful strategies for individual processing. When we choose activities for the learner *as a partner*, we provide opportunities for our students to express themselves in a safe environment and to meet for brief social interactions, which is so necessary for constructing knowledge. Making Connections and Partner Talks are two effective strategies to use when students work with partners. When we organize activities for the learner *as a member of a cooperative group*, we provide opportunities for students to learn negotiating and collaborating skills, and to be accountable to others. Numbered Heads Together and Jigsaw activities are engaging strategies for this type of small-group interaction. When we bring the whole class together, we provide opportunities for the learner *as a part of the larger classroom community*. It is in this large grouping that we create the environment and build the culture of a community of learners. We can use the Socratic Seminar and ReQuest strategies to model higher-level thinking for our students when we use the whole-class setting.

Consider a variety of grouping strategies that address the learner as an individual, a partner, a member of a small group, and a part of a larger class community.

■ MY LEARNING LOG • the learner as an individual

My Learning Log is a place where a student reflects upon what he or she has learned about a subject and about him- or herself as a learner. On their own or guided by the prompts provided on page 111, students ponder, predict, and evaluate what they've learned and how they've learned it.

The logs are easy to prepare; simply provide students with a copy of the reproducible learning log and have them place it in a folder or tape it to the first page of a notebook (make additional copies of the form for a folder or have students draw the same format on the next sheet of paper in their notebooks). You can assign students to write a daily or weekly log. Encourage them to record their thoughts about big ideas, connections, similarities and differences, confusing or difficult parts, and aha! moments that

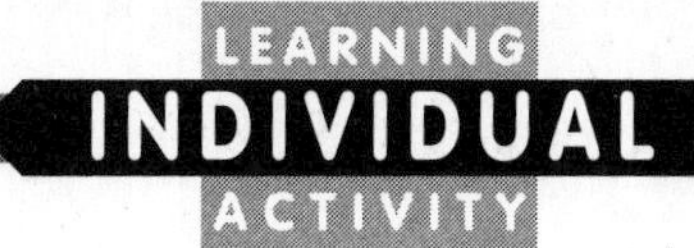

MY LEARNING LOG

Respond to one of the sentences below in your Learning Log:

- Make a connection to something you already know about the topic.
- Make a connection to something in your own life (note a similarity or a difference).
- Identify a confusing part. (What is the biggest difficulty you are having?)
- Is there a tip you can offer someone who is struggling with what you're learning?
- Determine what's most important to understand.
- Pose questions that you wonder about.
- Summarize what you have learned.
- Assess your progress so far in this unit of study.
- Note what you have learned about yourself as a learner.
- Set a goal for yourself. (What do you still want to know or be able to do?)

Date **Topic/Reading** **My Reflection**

they experience during reading, class discussion, or at other times. You might also guide them to assess their performance throughout the unit and set personal learning goals for themselves. Suggest that they choose different ways to respond to their learning by selecting a different prompt from the list each time they reflect in their log. By learning to self-assess, set goals for the future, and reflect upon their own learning process, students gain knowledge of themselves, their strengths, and their weaknesses.

Assessing the logs helps you tune into challenges students may be experiencing or misconceptions you can help them sort out. Collect the logs on a rotating basis and offer feedback to your students in the form of informal written comments, or use the logs to prepare yourself for one-on-one conferences with students.

My Opinions Journal becomes a reflection of how each student "comes to know." Using these journal entries, students personalize their learning and find more relevance in their studies.

■ MY OPINIONS JOURNAL • the learner as an individual

Another tool for helping students to reflect on their learning is **My Opinions Journal**. Using a small journal notebook, students record a belief that they hold about what they've learned. My Opinions Journal teaches students how to form an opinion, support it with evidence, and articulate it to others. One way to use this tool is at the beginning of a unit of study, to help students activate prior knowledge and make a personal connection to the material you will cover.

To help students focus on important concepts, first brainstorm the big ideas or key concepts in the unit as a class. Then, using the statement format *I believe* ____ *because* ____ as a model, ask them to state a belief that they hold about the ideas and provide support for their opinion with reasons, facts, examples, quotes, and so on. When students are comfortable with this format, stop periodically throughout a unit or activity and ask students to *form an opinion* about a particular concept, character, statement, or issue—and record it in their journal.

You may have to differentiate this task for some students by providing a written prompt to get them started (*I think the main character was a hero because...; I believe protecting endangered species is important because...*). Alternatively, you can make the task more challenging for advanced thinkers by asking these students to revisit opinions they have made about a particular topic and reflect on whether these opinions have changed and why. Over time, the journal will become a reflection of the way each individual thinks and how he or she "comes to know"—a visual tool for learners to really see what they think. Students will find more relevance in their studies and retain new information by personalizing their learning through these journal entries. See Figure 6.1 for an outline to use with students for their journals.

Figure 6.1

MY OPINIONS JOURNAL

To provide students with a structured format for this activity, use a model such as the outline below for recording their opinions.

Date **I believe**

____

____

____

____

To support this belief I offer the following facts, examples, statistics, quotes, ideas, etc.

____

____

____

____

■ PARTNER TALKS • the learner as a partner

Partner Talks are easy to integrate into daily lessons. Appealing to the social needs of most of our students, these short talk sessions give students the opportunity to list, share, compare, summarize, and elaborate upon information they've learned in class. For students who are shy about talking or reading in front of the whole class, partner work also provides a safe haven in which to share.

To initiate Partner Talks during a lesson, allow a brief time (three to five minutes) for partners to discuss key ideas they have learned about the topic or concept. Ask that both partners record these ideas in their notebooks, so that each remains focused on the task. While students talk and record, you have the opportunity to move about the room and work with pairs of students who may need further guidance in thinking about the material. Following the discussion, give students the choice of writing a verbal summary or creating a graphic, nonlinguistic representation of the information in their notebooks. This discussion strategy can provide a link between topics or closure at the end of a class period. My favorite way to use this strategy is to have partners discuss at the end of a lesson the answer to a focus question that I posed at the beginning of the lesson. Sometimes, I

TIP

Making Connections activity: Struggling learners may have difficulty coming up with terms and key phrases on their own. You can scaffold their work by providing them a list of terms (on labels or index cards) and ask students to work with their partners to group these terms, instead of completing steps 1 and 2 (see instructions on page 115). They will join the other students in the class at step 3.

have students write their answers on individual Exit Cards (see Chapter 2) after the Partner Talks in order to assess what they have learned.

Learning Partners can help each other in other ways, too. I like to use them for Partner Checks when I can't assess everyone's work or check that all students have accurately copied down their homework from the board. Having students turn to a partner to complete a task is an easy and effective grouping strategy that doesn't require a great deal of planning.

■ MAKING CONNECTIONS • the learner as a partner

Making Connections is a kinesthetic activity for partners that helps them synthesize their understandings about a unit using a combination of words and graphics. Using sticky notes and markers on construction paper, partners produce a graphic organizer that serves as an excellent visual tool for review.

Before you begin the activity, distribute copies of the Making Connections reproducible on page 115, and review the steps in the process with students. Encourage them to make connections between newly studied content and previously learned material and identify similarities and differences among concepts by comparing and classifying information. They will represent the content as pictures and symbols, wherever appropriate.

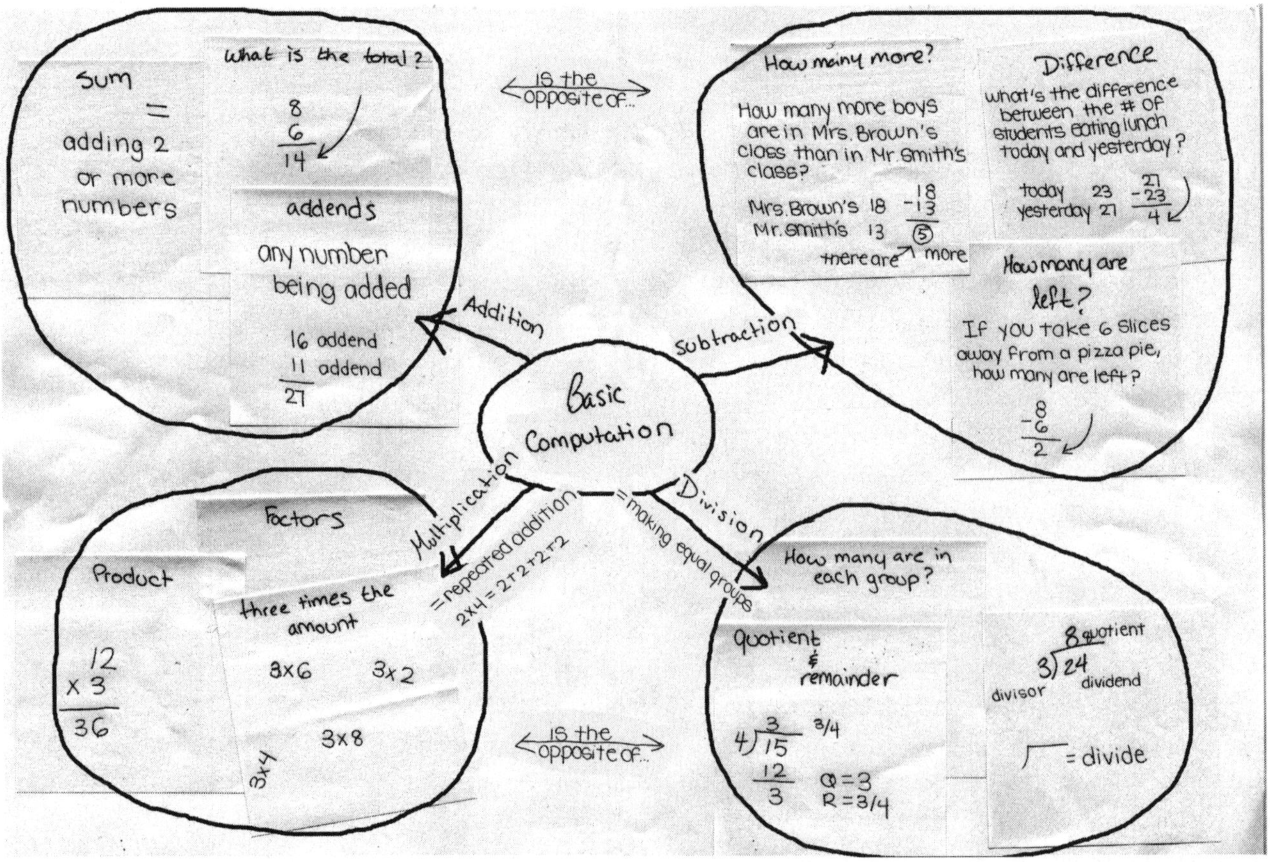

A Making Connections Collage helps two fourth graders make sense of the topic "basic computation." Students work together grouping and organizing terms, writing definitions, and creating and labeling examples to help themselves.

LEARNING PARTNER ACTIVITY

MAKING CONNECTIONS

Topic: ______________________________

You and your partner will create a graphic organizer that shows what you've both learned about this topic. You will each need ten sticky notes. You'll work together on a large sheet of paper with the sticky notes and colored markers.

STEP 1 On your own, list ten important terms/key phrases that come to mind when you think of this topic. Place one idea on each sticky note.

STEP 2 Pair with a partner. Share your ideas. If you find the same idea in your notes, keep just one copy of the sticky note.

STEP 3 Using the remaining sticky notes, group ideas that go together. The terms in each group must have something to do with one another.

On a large piece of construction paper, write the topic or title of what you are studying. Place the groups of terms (sticky notes) on the paper in a way that makes sense to you. Put a circle, box, or other design around each group of terms. Label each group. These groups are your subtopics. Define terms and give examples wherever you can.

Now, add any important terms about the topic that you feel are missing.

You can draw arrows and other design elements (bullets, color, pictures, etc.) to make your graphic organizer as clear and meaningful as possible.

STEP 4 Share the first draft of your organizer with another pair of classmates. Discuss your best ideas with them and listen as they share their organizer with you. Did they remember something you haven't included? Record any ideas that you may have forgotten on your first draft.

STEP 5 Return to work with your partner. Review your own organizer and add any new ideas to your final draft.

STEP 6 Share what you've learned by giving an oral presentation or displaying your organizer.

STEP 7 (Optional) Generate a class organizer by gleaning the best ideas from all the groups.

■ NUMBERED HEADS TOGETHER • the learner as part of a small group

Numbered Heads Together is a group strategy based on the work of Spencer Kagan (1994). Although there are many variations of this cooperative structure, they all involve small groups of students working together to ensure that every member of their team can answer a question, solve a problem, or complete a given task. You might pose a question about a reading assignment, present a math problem, or ask students to create an awareness campaign for recycling. This strategy can be used with any grade level or subject area. There are numerous benefits, including the opportunity for students to rehearse information, learn from one another, build individual accountability in a group, engage in a high degree of activity, and receive support at all levels so that the questions or tasks can be appropriately challenging.

To begin this activity, place students in mixed-ability groups, and number them off from one to four. Provide a question, problem, or task, and tell students to "put your heads together and make sure everyone in your group can answer the question (or solve the problem or complete the task)." Since this is a mixed-ability grouping, expect that some students will initially be able to respond more quickly than others; remind these students to help their peers. Be sure to provide enough wait time so that peer teaching can take place and all members of each group can become prepared. Then, call a number (from one to four) and have the appropriate member of each group provide the answer out loud or complete the task on the board, without any assistance from their teammates. You can give a point to each team whose member responds correctly and add the total number of points to an upcoming assessment for each student in the group.

When you use this cooperative learning strategy to review a unit of study, you place more responsibility in the hands of your students. One teacher I worked with had each group create a web on which they brainstormed everything they knew about a particular subtopic or concept prior

Figure 6.2

NUMBERED HEADS TOGETHER

- Carefully watch the groups at work to be sure you have provided enough wait time for group members to help one another.
- If time allows, before you announce the question, problem, or task, have each student brainstorm ideas about a subtopic or concept on a group web. This will help them to activate prior knowledge.
- You might have the students who are selected to answer write on a "response board" (a small chalkboard, dry-erase board, or laminated poster paper) that they can all hold up when prompted. Or have students go up to the blackboard and write responses at the same time.

to her posing a series of questions. This gave students the opportunity to work together to activate prior knowledge and focus on key understandings. The graphic organizer helped the visual learners see what they had learned. The group interaction helped the interpersonal learners learn from one another. The mixed-ability grouping promoted positive interdependence among members because by the end of the task, each member had to be able to respond appropriately. Her lesson was one of the most engaging differentiated review sessions I have ever seen. See Figure 6.2 for ideas on implementing this strategy.

I like to use the Jigsaw method because it makes students more responsible for their own learning. It also allows me to move around and help small groups of students.

—FIFTH-GRADE TEACHER

■ THE JIGSAW CLASSROOM • the learner as a part of a small group

Based on the work of Elliot Aronson et al. (1978), the Jigsaw method is a cooperative structure that holds each student accountable for the success of his or her small group. Beginning in a "home group," each of four students is assigned one subtopic of a unit, chapter, or research topic, or a particular category of information. The four subtopics of a Civil War unit might be the Causes of the War, the Advantages of the North and South, the Abolitionist Movement, and Reconstruction. The four categories of information in a short stories unit might be Characterization, Setting, Conflicts, and Themes. After receiving their assignment, all students move to "expert groups," where they work with others who have the same assignment and develop a strategy for sharing what they have "come to know" back in their home group. This might include developing a top-ten list, a rhyme, a graphic organizer, a model, or any other appropriate way to show the information and ideas students have generated. Applicable to all content areas and appropriate for students in grades four and beyond, the Jigsaw method exemplifies "cooperation by design" (Aronson, 2000)—it facilitates peer interaction and leads students to value each other as contributors to their common task.

TIP

Assign struggling students the same number (section or subtopic) in each group. This way, when they move to their **expert groups,** they will be together, and you will be able to work with several of these students and provide them with additional support.

Here are the steps I use to lead a basic Jigsaw activity. (See Figure 6.3, The Jigsaw Sequence, for a visual of how the groups break down and move.)

1. *Place students in heterogeneous home groups of four.* (Keep groups diverse in terms of gender, ethnicity, race, and ability.)
2. *Divide the lesson into four segments*, assigning one member of the group to each segment. To differentiate this activity based on readiness, you can place any struggling students in the same expert group (e.g., they are all number 3 in their group) and assign this group a subtopic that is less complex, such as identifying the settings found in several short stories for a study of story elements. At the same time, you might assign advanced readers to an expert group with a subtopic that requires higher-level thinking, such as comparing the themes found in several short stories.

3. *Have students move to expert groups,* where they will work with others to master the same segment and rehearse a presentation that they will make to their home groups. (Allow about 15 minutes.) If you have differentiated this activity based on readiness, as suggested in Step 2, you will have several struggling learners in the same group. You can move to this group and provide them with the extra assistance they need to complete their task.
4. *Have students return to their home groups,* where each student presents his or her segment to the group. Others listen, ask questions to clarify information, and take notes. (Allow 20 minutes.)
5. *Give a quiz or other short assessment* at the end of the session, or the next day, to hold students accountable for the information.

There are as many variations of the Jigsaw Classroom as there are creative teachers, but they all promote positive interdependence while ensuring individual accountability. The Jigsaw method allows for socialization and is, therefore, a developmentally appropriate strategy for students in the middle grades. It encourages active listening, social engagement, and empathy among classmates as well, because each student depends on the other to complete his or her learning task.

Figure 6.3

The Jigsaw Sequence

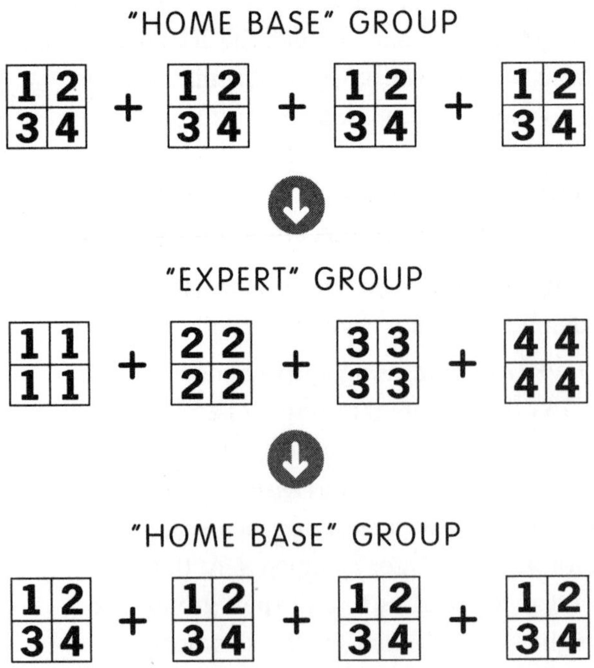

"HOME BASE" GROUP

12/34 + 12/34 + 12/34 + 12/34

↓

"EXPERT" GROUP

11/11 + 22/22 + 33/33 + 44/44

↓

"HOME BASE" GROUP

12/34 + 12/34 + 12/34 + 12/34

If you are implementing the Jigsaw strategy for the first time, be patient. Since it is a complex structure, it may not work as smoothly as you'd like at first. Understand that it places high expectations and responsibility on students and requires good management skills, which you'll develop over time (you might want to ask an aide or parent volunteer to help with monitoring groups when you begin). Stick with it; research has shown that students become more confident learners, like school better, and achieve more academically through the use of this cooperative strategy. It's worth the initial effort to make it a part of your classroom design. See Figure 6.4 for tips on how to make the Jigsaw activity work for you.

Figure 6.4

JIGSAW ACTIVITY

- When students are working in their groups, move from group to group, observing the process and making any necessary interventions.
- Assign one group leader, whose job it is to call on students and make sure all students participate evenly in the sharing.
- Have the class evaluate the process. Provide the following questions to each student on a rubric with a scale of one to four: Did you listen actively? Did you encourage other group members? Did you contribute positively to your group's success? Did your group do its best job? Share students' responses as a class. Discuss what individuals or groups might need to do differently next time.
- If your expert groups are too large, you can split them into two separate groups working on the same topic.
- Closely monitor the expert groups, making sure that students who struggle with listening or note-taking have an accurate report to bring back to their home group. (If you have placed struggling learners in the same expert group, you or an aide can provide scaffolding in the form of written notes, a vocabulary bank, or guided questions.)
- You might want students in the expert groups to prepare a mini-poster (containing important facts, information, and diagrams) to assist them in their home-group presentations.
- Provide each student with a Jigsaw worksheet, chart, or graphic organizer to record what they learn as they listen back in their home groups. This will become a study sheet for students. (See page 120.)

online connection

Visit the official Jigsaw Web site to learn more about the Jigsaw Classroom. This site includes an account from Professor Aronson, who originated the strategy.

http://www.jigsaw.org/index.html

JIGSAW WORKSHEET

Topic: ______________________________

1 (Subtopic): ____________________

Write key ideas that you learn below:

→ ______________________________

____

→ ______________________________

____

→ ______________________________

____

→ ______________________________

____

2 (Subtopic): ____________________

Write key ideas that you learn below:

→ ______________________________

____

→ ______________________________

____

→ ______________________________

____

→ ______________________________

____

3 (Subtopic): ____________________

Write key ideas that you learn below:

→ ______________________________

____

→ ______________________________

____

→ ______________________________

____

→ ______________________________

____

4 (Subtopic): ____________________

Write key ideas that you learn below:

→ ______________________________

____

→ ______________________________

____

→ ______________________________

____

→ ______________________________

____

■ SOCRATIC SEMINARS • the learner as part of a large group

"To what extent does the Bill of Rights impact your life personally—totally, greatly, minimally, or not at all?" As students in your class ponder the answer to that question, they focus on the document in front of them. The conversation that ensues is lively, with students always citing evidence from the text (the Bill of Rights), frequently asking questions of one another, sometimes disagreeing with one another, and occasionally changing their minds because of someone else's point of view.

In the Socratic approach to teaching, the teacher poses thoughtful questions to help students explore ideas, issues, and values in their text readings. Socratic Seminars foster active learning, critical thinking, and improved reading skills. Seated in a circle, students are encouraged to think for themselves and to explain their thinking as they respond to open-ended questions initially posed by the teacher and then by their peers. The teacher acts as a facilitator, helping students to stay focused on the text, clarify their positions, and keep the flow of conversation going.

Socratic Seminars also promote team building and appropriate classroom behavior. Students are taught to look at one another when they speak and listen, to wait their turn to respond, and to communicate in a way that shows respect for viewpoints differing from their own. Through rigorous and thoughtful dialogue, students are encouraged to articulate their ideas, to seek deeper understanding of complex concepts, and, always, to return to the text to find evidence and support for their ideas.

To ensure that the Socratic Seminar runs smoothly, you may want to scaffold the lesson at each stage of learning—before, during, and after the group discussion.

Figure 6.5

FOUR ELEMENTS OF A SOCRATIC SEMINAR

- *The text* may be readings (poem, short story, essay, or document) from any discipline or works of art or music.
- *The questions* are high level, often student generated, and reflect genuine curiosity.
- *The leader* poses the focus question and then serves in a dual role as leader and participant.
- *The participants* study the text in advance, listen actively, share their ideas, and find evidence in the text to support their beliefs.

TIP

A **QuickWrite** is a timed written reflection that helps students activate prior knowledge about the ideas, issues, or values contained in the reading. (It will be particularly important for your visual learners to use this opportunity to write down terms they may need to use during the seminar conversation. In fact, you can provide key terms on the board for them to use in their QuickWrites. This will help support students with auditory memory problems to keep track of the discussion.)

Pre-seminar:

Follow the steps below to activate prior knowledge, increase student motivation and interest, and help students make personal connections to the text.

1. *Assign the text reading ahead of time* or provide a few minutes for students to read, share thoughts with a partner, and record a few ideas using the Jot-Pair-Share or QuickWrite strategy. (See Chapter 2, Stop and Process activities, and the tip on this page.)
2. *Formulate a set of high-level open-ended questions.* Eventually you can have students create their own questions, demonstrating a constructivist approach to inquiry. (See Chapter 4, Questions in Bloom.)
3. Distribute copies of the Socratic Resource Page on page 124 to the class. Make a special point of referring your visual learners to the list of questions that will help them to focus during this auditory strategy. (Note: As the seminar proceeds, periodically write summary notes reflecting student contributions on the chalkboard or overhead. Remind visual learners especially to copy the summary notes into their notebooks so they will have something concrete to refer to during any follow-up activities you may assign. See Things to Consider: Socratic Seminars, on page 123.)

During the seminar:

Use one of the following strategies to encourage participation, help keep students focused, and establish an even pace of questioning.

Speaking Chips: Hand out an equal number of chips to all participants at the beginning of the seminar. Encourage students to use one of their chips each time they add to the discussion. This helps students who participate more actively to pace themselves, while encouraging more reticent students to become engaged.

Linking Ideas: Ask each participant (in turn) for a contribution. Students may pass. Encourage them to use one of the following prompts when contributing or answering a question:

- I believe. . . and here in the text it says. . .
- I agree with (name of student) because. . . and here in the text it says. . .
- I disagree with (name of student) because. . . and here in the text it says. . .

Post-seminar:

Offer students the following choices as a way for them to reflect on what they've learned and personalize the information.

My Learning Log: Have students self-assess their participation in the seminar and set future learning goals (see pages 110 and 111).

My Opinions Journal: Have students identify and articulate personal perspectives about the ideas, issues, and values discussed (see pages 113 and 114).

Seminar Self-Assessment: Encourage students to ask themselves the following questions. (You might post them on chart paper or have students make their own checklists.)

Did I. . .

- come to the seminar prepared with notes, text, and questions?
- participate fully?
- offer comments, without prompting, to move the conversation forward?
- listen to others respectfully?
- paraphrase accurately?
- ask for help when I was unclear about something?
- use the text to find support?

Time to share: Invite students to share their reflections with one another as a whole class.

Things to Consider: Socratic Seminars

Have I

❍ modeled higher-level questioning by posing open-ended questions that ask my students to analyze, evaluate, speculate, judge, and defend?

❍ encouraged students to express their diverse viewpoints by asking if anyone has a different opinion from the one that's been expressed?

❍ invited elaboration by asking *students to clarify their statements?*

❍ encouraged all students to participate by using the Speaking Chips and Linking Ideas strategies (page 122)?

❍ allowed a five- to ten-second wait time, giving students time to reflect before I respond?

❍ periodically summarized on the board or overhead to help visual learners process what has been discussed?

online connection

Visit this site for basic information, types of questions, guidelines for participants, and rubrics you can use with Socratic Seminars.

http://www.studyguide.org/socratic_seminar.htm

Visit this site for a description of how to run a Socratic Seminar in a middle-school class.

http://www.middleweb.com/Socratic.html

SOCRATIC SEMINAR RESOURCE PAGE

Tips for a great conversation:

- ✔ Listen to each other carefully.
- ✔ Talk to each other, not just the teacher or leader.
- ✔ Paraphrase another's ideas before responding either in support or disagreement (I agree/disagree with ____'s idea that… because…).
- ✔ Always refer back to the text to support your ideas.
- ✔ Whenever you don't understand what someone has said, ask for clarification.
- ✔ Do not interrupt another speaker.
- ✔ Do not raise your hand to be called on; take turns speaking.

To keep the conversation flowing and focused during the seminar, here are some great questions that you can ask your classmates:

What is your main point?

Can you give me an example?

What's your view and how did you arrive at it?

Can you show me (in the text) where the proof is?

Why do you say that?

What are you assuming?

Are there any other conclusions we could draw?

What effect would that have?

What does that remind you of?

Can you compare this with anything else we have learned/read about?

Why would someone consider this to be bad (or good)?

What do you predict will happen in the future?

■ THE ReQuest STRATEGY • the learner as part of a large group

The most appropriate time to introduce something new to all students is when the whole class is together. ReQuest, a reciprocal questioning strategy, models for students in a large group how to analyze a text and improve their comprehension of the new material (Manzo, 1969). Most appropriate for students in grades five and up, this reading-questioning procedure works like a mini-workshop and provides guided practice for students in developing purposeful questions about their reading. The goal of this comprehension-centered activity is to help students get meaning from their reading and to move students beyond low-level, literal understanding to higher-order thinking.

To implement this strategy, first choose a section of any fiction or nonfiction text that both you and your students will read at the same time. Then, close your book and have your students formulate questions to ask you about the reading. At first, they will tend to ask text-explicit questions with answers that are easy to find in the text, such as *What is a circuit? Who discovered electricity? When was electricity discovered?* You will reinforce strategic reading by answering the questions and showing students where you found the answers. Next, have students close their books and begin to model for them probing, higher-level questions. Ask them questions that require them to use inference or more complex thought to answer. *What safety rules can you design to protect young children around electricity? What would life be like if there were no electricity? How does life now compare with life in the 1600s?* Students will observe your question patterns and learn, over time, to think critically and analyze information on their own.

online connection

Visit this site to see how the ReQuest strategy for increasing reading comprehension can be used as a game in the classroom.

http://www.angelfire.com/ak/teacherpage/gam4.html

I use the following steps to help students learn to generate their own higher-level thinking questions for making sense of their reading:

1. Distribute copies of the text to students and have them read it silently. (Make sure you read the text carefully as well.) Assign a manageable amount of reading (one to five paragraphs), depending upon students' grade level and comprehension abilities. (Differentiate this task by allowing weak readers to read with a reading partner.)
2. Put your copy of the book or passage aside and invite students to ask you questions about the text.

3. Reinforce student learning by answering the questions and explaining how you got the answer (through prior knowledge, by noting what was directly stated in the text, by putting together ideas found in different places in the text, by drawing conclusions through inference, etc.).
4. Exchange roles with students: have students put aside their texts; now it's your turn to question students about the same reading and model higher level and more inferential questions.
5. Repeat the process with the next part of the text.

This quick-paced modeling strategy is designed to engage the whole class. Through peer interaction and the constant interchange of questions and answers between students and the teacher, multiple perspectives of the same topic are bound to evolve. This social construction of knowledge contributes to students' understanding of the reading. The modeling you provide and the peer learning that takes place give students comprehension tools to use when they read independently.

Things to Consider: ReQuest Strategy

Did I

❍ model for students how I got my answer?

❍ model questions that require students to consider different parts of the text to answer? (*How did the main character change over time?*)

❍ differentiate my questions (using Bloom's Taxonomy—see Chapter 4) according to students' reading readiness?

❍ ask questions that help students analyze, speculate, evaluate, and support with evidence? (What attributes do you believe were most important to Buck's survival in the wilderness?)

As you begin to implement the suggestions in this chapter, you may find yourself shifting from using one predominant classroom arrangement to a more flexible arrangement that supports moving in and out of whole class, partners, small groups, and needs-based groups on a regular basis. Having taken the time necessary to prepare students to work effectively in flexible groupings, you are now ready to have student groups work on different tasks at the same time. These groups will be able to meet the readiness needs of your students by providing appropriate challenges for them. In the next chapter, you will see why setting the stage with flexible groups is so critical for making tiered lessons work for you and your students.

PRINCIPLES OF EFFECTIVE INSTRUCTION EXPLORED IN THIS CHAPTER:

Ongoing and frequent assessments

•

Respect for all types of learners

•

Reducing anxiety

•

Flexible groupings

•

Lessons designed around the "big ideas"

•

Scaffolding for struggling learners

•

Challenge for advanced learners

CHAPTER 7

Tiering Lessons

Tiering lessons is an essential part of a differentiated classroom. A tiered lesson addresses students' readiness: we match an instructional task with a student's skills and understanding of the subject or topic. As students work on different tasks, they all focus on the same essential understandings and skills, but at different levels of complexity, abstractness, and open-endedness (Tomlinson, 1999). The time to consider tiering a lesson is when you realize that some of your students have already mastered an important concept while others have still not grasped the basics. You need not tier a lesson for every concept. Instead, you decide to tier a lesson when the concept is *critical* to understanding and moving ahead. In this era of assessments, your tiered lesson most likely will be assessment related. See Figure 7.1 for additional thoughts about when to tier an assignment.

I have placed the chapter on tiering assignments last because I believe that tiering is the most difficult strategy to implement when you are beginning to differentiate your classroom. The preceding chapters prepare you to create tiered lessons by expanding your instructional strategies in these areas:

- gathering information on what students already know about a particular concept so that you can plan appropriate instruction (see Stop-and-Process Activities in Chapter 2);

- responding to student interest by providing them with opportunities to choose learning tasks that appeal to their intellectual strengths (see Chapters 3 and 5);
- developing more complex and rigorous tasks to challenge students to think critically (see Chapters 4 and 5);
- using a number of grouping scenarios to maximize the teaching and learning process. If we are able to handle the management of frequently changing flexible groups, we can more successfully run multiple activities at the same time (see Chapter 6).

Having built this background, we are now ready to tier lessons that provide appropriate challenge to students at different levels of readiness.

Figure 7.1

WHEN SHOULD I TIER AN ASSIGNMENT?

When **some** students

❍ are ready to move ahead and other students need more time.

❍ would benefit from using different resources, readings, or materials to understand the basic concepts.

❍ need more modeling and direct instruction.

❍ need more challenge, more independence, or more complexity.

All of us do not have equal talents, but all of us should have an equal opportunity to develop our talents.

JOHN F. KENNEDY

Show Me the Research!

When we look for research that supports the use of tiering as an instructional strategy, we first look to the work of Lev Vygotsky, a Russian psychologist whose early twentieth-century work on child development provides a cornerstone for best-practice instruction today. Vygotsky suggested that a child works best in his or her "zone of proximal development" (ZPD), where, with the help of an adult or in collaboration with more capable peers, the child can accomplish a task that he or she cannot perform independently (1978, 1986).

According to Vygotsky, the role of education is to provide children with experiences that are in their ZPD, activities that challenge children but which they can accomplish with guidance and scaffolding. Educators create these learning opportunities by structuring the learning task and the surrounding environment so that the demands on the child are at an appropriately challenging level, and by constantly adjusting the amount of adult intervention to meet the child's changing needs and abilities (Berk & Winsler, 1995).

In a Vygotskian model, a teacher provides assistance when a student needs help and gradually reduces the amount of assistance as the student gains competence. This responsive interaction offers appropriate challenges for each learner. By keeping tasks slightly above the level of their students' independent functioning, teachers can "rouse to life" the cognitive processes that are developing in their students (Tharp & Gallimore, 1988). For instance, a teacher might provide direct instruction to a small group of students who needs help completing a math task such as rounding to the tens place. After modeling how to complete one of the problems, the teacher might guide the group through solving a second similar problem and then ask the students to walk him or her through a third problem. Depending on the students' facility with rounding at this point, the teacher may give the students several problems to try independently and check their completed work. Those students who have mastered the rounding skill are sent off to continue work independently while those who still have trouble remain with the teacher for review. Once they have mastered the skill, they are ready to work on their own, and the teacher will send them off for independent practice.

All students are gifted; some just open their packages earlier than others.

UNKNOWN

Providing the right amount of challenge is critical to making tiered assignments worthwhile. Putting students into groups to work on a task that either they have already mastered or is far beyond their readiness makes no sense. Jensen (1996) points out that the best learning state is in between boredom and anxiety. Sousa (2001) recommends a "moderate challenge" for optimal learning to take place. Bransford, Brown, and Cocking (1999, 2000) make the case for designing student tasks at an appropriate level of difficulty. "Tasks that are too easy become boring; tasks that are too difficult cause frustration." If we are to maximize learning for students and ensure academic growth, we must present material that is *above*, not at or below, students' mastery level. At the same time, the material we present must not be *too far* above the zone of proximal development for these students, or we risk confusing and frustrating them (Byrnes, 1996).

Brain researchers agree that learning occurs when the brain is neither over- nor under-challenged. Through their latest research, we have come to understand that the human brain is so unique that any lockstep group instruction is unlikely to meet the needs of most learners (Jensen, 1996). Teaching to the human brain means teachers must provide greater choice for learners and diversity in instruction. Drawing upon the work of Vygotsky and others, we have come to understand that the need for appropriate challenge and motivation of learners can be met through tiered lessons.

Putting Research Into Action

Tomlinson refers to tiered lessons as the "the meat and potatoes" of a differentiated classroom (Tomlinson, 1999). In fact, until we tier lessons in our classrooms, we will not be addressing one of the most important differences in our students—that of student readiness. To get the most out of a differentiated classroom and to truly be responsive to student needs, we *must tier instruction* according to the brain-based research introduced by Vygotsky and espoused by Sousa, Jensen, and others.

Tomlinson prefers to use the term *mixed-readiness* to the more traditional term *mixed-ability*. Readiness—the current knowledge, understanding, and skill level a student has related to a particular concept—can and does change. Tomlinson makes the case that with sufficient scaffolding and assistance, all students can achieve at unexpected levels. Tiered lessons provide the perfect format to offer this support to students at different levels without pigeonholing any particular student into a fixed level of challenge. Through tiered lessons, teachers can help *all* students to stretch a manageable amount and provide them support as they do so. (Tomlinson & Cunningham Edison, 2003).

Tomlinson suggests that there are many ways to provide appropriate challenges to learners at all levels. By recognizing each learner's starting point, we can plan tasks that move along a continuum (something she calls an "equalizer") and fine-tune our classroom instruction with individual learners by moving, for example, from single-step to multistep tasks, from concrete information to more abstract ideas and concepts, from structured activities to more open-ended tasks, from teacher-directed skill building to self-guided independent work, and from slow-paced study to fast-paced instruction (2001).

RELATED LITERATURE

For additional ideas on the development of tiered lessons, read Carol Ann Tomlinson's *The Differentiated Classroom: Responding to the Needs of All Learners* (ASCD, 1999) and *How to Differentiate Instruction in Mixed-Ability Classrooms* (ASCD, 2001).

In my experience, the group of students least challenged in heterogeneous classrooms is the advanced group of learners. Unless placed in "cluster groupings," where several high achievers are placed together in the same class, the advanced learner's needs often go unmet. A study conducted by the National Research Center on the Gifted and Talented shows that cluster grouping can raise achievement for *all* children and even increase the number of students identified as high achievers. In such classrooms, teachers are encouraged to plan and design curriculum to meet the specific needs of advanced learners. Too often, however, the teacher in a heterogeneous classroom has only one, two, or three advanced learners in a large class. The teacher, therefore, concentrates on planning for the rest of the class, believing that the advanced learners will be fine on their own. In fact, they often become disillusioned with school, frustrated, and bored with the pace. Sometimes, they become discipline problems.

In an ASCD Education Update, Tomlinson (2004) reminds us that "we would never take our best basketball player and say he or she doesn't need a coach to become successful." In much the same way, she points out, our most able students need good instruction from their teacher. Advanced students, as much as other students, need to be coached along to reach their full potential. By using tiered lessons, we can accommodate the advanced learner, challenge the on-grade learner, and at the same time scaffold the struggling learner.

Figure 7.2

SCAFFOLDING FOR STRUGGLING LEARNERS

When students struggle with skills and concepts, provide them with

- more modeling, additional teacher instruction, review of concepts, peer tutoring
- color-coded elements, highlighted elements, exemplars of writing or assessments
- manipulatives, sentence strips, sticky notes, flash cards, address labels typed with vocabulary terms, access to text resources
- more opportunities to use language: vocabulary lists, cards with pictures, word banks, opportunities to discuss the topic using provided terms, word walls, lists of questions, a list of signal words
- a graphic organizer, an incomplete outline, a framed paragraph, sentence starters, prompts
- a template, a set of steps, a formula

Strategies

The strategies that follow will help you run successful tiered lessons. You'll learn multiple ways to design two or three different tasks around the same concept and find ways to make tiering invisible so there are few, if any, social problems related to the differences students notice among the leveled assignments. You'll also discover how to decide when to tier a lesson. And finally, you'll find lots of how-to tips for making it all run smoothly.

TEACHER REFLECTION

I decided to use tiered activities in my inclusion class, where I have gifted students as well. After setting the stage with several discussions about how we all have different strengths and weaknesses, my students accepted the idea that they would be working on different activities from their peers from time to time. I've tried to make the tiering "invisible" by assigning a similar-looking product to all students. For example, when I assign students to write a story, I give each group different story elements to include, which involves different levels of complexity. The best part of this activity is that all students are challenged appropriately for their readiness level in writing. They are all proud of their writing and in the end, we put all of the stories together in a class book.

—ELEMENTARY-SCHOOL TEACHER

■ TIERING FOR DIFFERENT LEVELS OF LEARNERS

There are many ways to design tiered lessons, with some teachers choosing to design up to five versions of one task. However, designing *two to three* versions of an activity is a reasonable goal and more than adequate in most classrooms. When you create a tiered activity, first identify the essential understandings and skills you want all students to learn. Then design an activity for *on-level learners* that clearly focuses student learning and causes them to make use of a key skill or skills to meet the learning objectives you've identified. Next, design a similar activity for your *struggling learners*, providing them with scaffolding (additional support, materials, or instruction). Figure 7.2 offers a variety of ways to provide assistance to struggling learners.

Finally, develop a third, more complex activity for your *advanced learners*. Be sure the activity is more complex, not simply more work. Diane Heacox (2002) suggests using questions derived from the work of Grant Wiggins and Jay McTighe to guide the planning of more-complex instruction. Use the questions below as a guide to plan more-complex activities in a tiered lesson.

Things to Consider: Leveling for Complexity

When creating tiered assignments and advanced tasks based on complexity, have I made sure to have students

- ❍ identify assumptions, points of view, or problems?
- ❍ examine and support their ideas, positions, conclusions, and perspectives?
- ❍ formulate, hypothesize, or synthesize new ideas?
- ❍ represent, model, or demonstrate ideas in a *new way* rather than simply listing, applying, or summarizing another's ideas?
- ❍ identify implications?
- ❍ explore "what if" scenarios or alternative perspectives, actions, or results?

(Based on the work of Heacox, 2002, and Wiggins and McTighe, 1998)

You can design your tiers based on Bloom's levels of challenge (see Chapter 4) or by complexity of the task. Using Bloom at lower to middle levels of challenge, you might ask students to identify information and create a chart, poster, or collage to illustrate their understanding (application level). At higher levels, you might construct a task that asks students to extend what they know about the information by comparing and contrasting it to something else they have learned (analysis).

Using complexity of the task to design tiered lessons, you might design a basic and an advanced version of the same task. The following tasks are basic and advanced versions of an activity taken from a science unit on recycling. Note that the tasks are built around the essential understandings that all students must learn—the types and benefits of recycling—regardless of the level of the task they complete.

Basic Task: Create an informational brochure to inform your classmates about several types of recycling in your school (or community). Include a list of the benefits of recycling.

Advanced Task: Create an informational brochure about an ideal school recycling program. In your brochure, suggest *at least one new way* to involve your peers in the program to recycle. Present a convincing argument about the benefits of your new program in your brochure.

In these examples, all students are asked to research a topic and design an informational brochure. However, the second, more advanced activity requires more complex research, greater independence, and drawing conclusions through analysis. The task is also more transformational, requiring students to stretch and create new ideas and then present them persuasively.

Whether a student is at a basic, on-grade, or advanced level, he should be pushed a bit beyond his comfort level and provided with support to reach the next level of competency. It is in this way that students gain a sense of self-efficacy, the pride that comes from accomplishing something they previously felt was unattainable.

Teachers are those who use themselves as bridges over which they invite their students to cross; then, having facilitated their crossing, joyfully collapse, encouraging them to create bridges of their own.

NIKOS KAZANTZAKIS, GREEK WRITER, POET, PHILOSOPHER

■ MAKING TIERING INVISIBLE

Probably one of the most important things for you to consider as you begin to implement tiered assignments in your classroom is how you will make tiering invisible. The biggest fear most teachers have about tiering is that students will feel it is unfair that they have been assigned an activity that appears different from their classmates' assignments. You can avoid such problems by preparing your students in two ways. First, make sure your students are used to moving in and out of different grouping arrangements that will make them comfortable in a classroom where more than one activity is going on at the same time. If your students are constantly moving in and out of cooperative groups, pairs, circles, needs groupings, Half-Class/Half-Class, and whole-class arrangements, they will be less concerned about a particular day's grouping for a tiered lesson. (See Chapter 6 for instructional strategies for flexible groupings.) Second, begin to introduce the concept of tiering by explaining to your students as Tomlinson and others have put it: "Fair is not equal. Fair is getting what you need."

KEY IDEA

Help students understand that "fair is not equal—fair is getting what you need."

To help students understand this concept, I engage students in a sharing activity called Identifying My Strengths. I ask students to draw a web with the words "my strengths" in the center. I model the activity on the board by showing them a web of my strengths. Then, I ask them to think about what they love to do or are good at doing both at school and at home. They write at least four subjects, hobbies, and/or other strengths on the spokes of their web, as shown in the example below. You might want to brainstorm a list with your class to help them focus on specific areas (participating in class, completing homework on time, helping others, reading for information, writing essays, writing poetry, analyzing charts and graphs, inventing things, etc.). Next, I ask them to share with their Learning Partners what they've recorded to discover how they are similar to and/or different from each other. As individual students share their strengths with the whole class, they come to understand that everyone has strengths in certain areas and also needs support in different areas. I tell them that at times, different students will be engaged in different activities because that's what they'll need. I explain that my job is to make sure that each student gets what he or she needs to be successful.

Identifying My Strengths

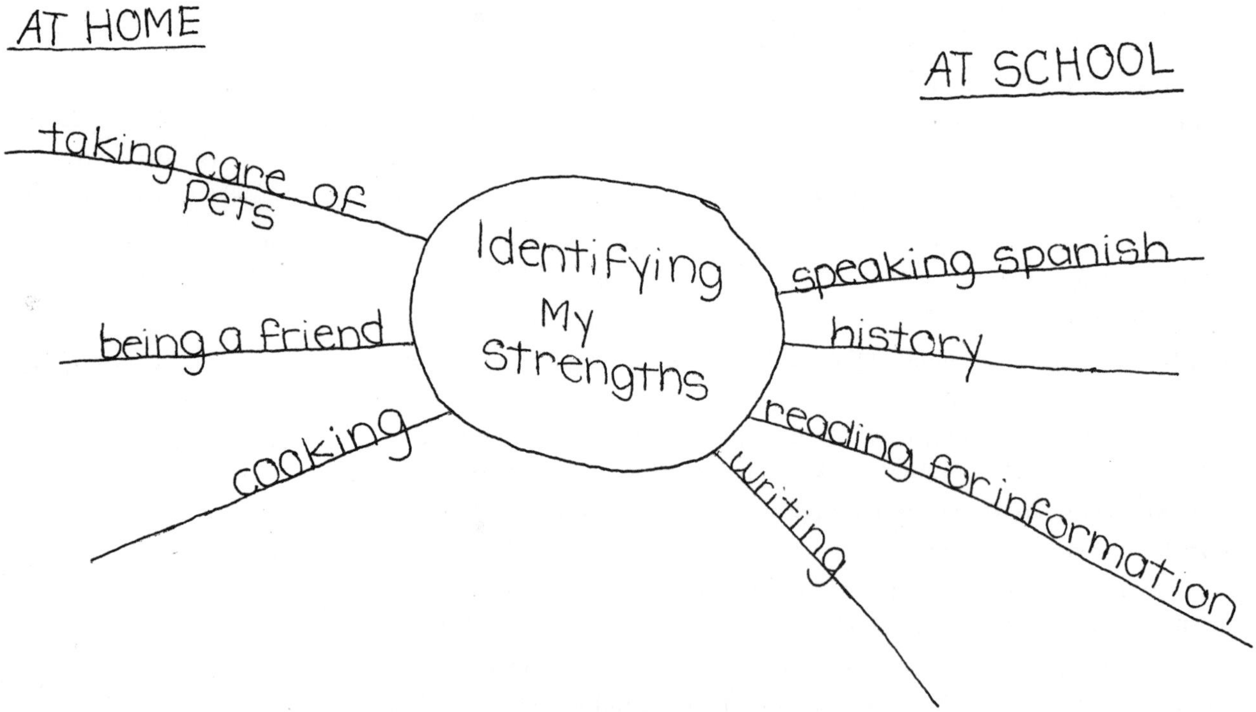

A student identifies her strengths using a web format. When students compare their webs, they see how everyone has different abilities and, therefore, different needs.

Having established that everyone's needs are different and, therefore, that students will occasionally be working on different tasks, you must be sure to make all tasks equally engaging, important, and fair. An advanced student should not be doing *more of the same kind of work* as a peer at a lower level of readiness. He or she should be doing more-rigorous thinking at higher levels of complexity. Conversely, a struggling learner should not be engaged in a paper-and-pencil task while advanced learners are actively creating a skit or preparing for a debate.

Try to design similar-looking activities or products across the levels. For instance, all students may be using maps. In a tiered assignment, one group of students writes a set of directions between two towns (application), while another group determines the types of occupations and recreational opportunities that may be found in a certain town and writes a "Job Opportunities and Recreation" Web page for the town's Web site (analysis). Or all students may be working to complete a one-page newsletter on Colonial times. In a tiered assignment, one group must include a list of job opportunities available to settlers in Jamestown (application), while another group must design a classified ad citing benefits for English settlers to come to the Southern colonies (analysis). At the end of the lesson, the teacher brings everyone together to share what they've learned and/or created. These tiered activities allow students to work at different levels of complexity. Yet, all students benefit from hearing the results of everyone's work.

Oral questioning, written journal prompts, objective tests, webbing, K-W-L chart (What do you **know**? What do you still **want** to know? What did you **learn**?), group discussions, and brainstorming sessions provide rich data about students' existing schema, including critical misconceptions.

BRANSFORD, BROWN, & COCKING

■ USING DATA TO TIER LESSONS

An important decision that you will need to make is how to assign students to a task geared to their individual learning needs. Using pre-assessment data that you can collect from a variety of sources, you can make decisions about how to group your students for tiered learning activities. In an age of standards, it is critically important that every lesson support student's learning and mastery of the objective you've targeted; an appropriately leveled task can lead a student to lesson mastery. Assessment data is key to your planning.

You have several choices about how to gather such data. Sometimes, you may group students based on ongoing observations and subjective assessments such as anecdotal and conference notes taken over the course of several independent work periods. When you have an activity that requires students to use a specific set of skills such as writing a summary paragraph, you may want to present a basic mini-lesson to students and then give a quick assessment like an Exit Card or a QuickWrite for an immediate evaluation of their ability to handle the task (see Chapter 2). If you are assigning activities that require background knowledge or prerequisite skills, you may want to give a pre-assessment task before you begin a lesson or unit. Based on the results, you would assign students a particular level of activity.

A more student-centered approach that works well for me and many of my upper-grade colleagues is to let *students* choose which task to work on, based on their own self-assessment. I find that most of the time, students tend to be extremely honest in their assessments. If you decide to let students choose which activity to work on, you might call the tiered activities by name (or "Tasks A, B, and C," as below) and provide some guidance for students by saying and posting the following:

"If you're not quite sure about_____, choose Task A_____."

"If you're starting to understand_____ but need a little more practice, choose Task B_____."

"If you completely understand_____ and can teach it to someone else, choose Task C_____."

Everyone is ignorant, only on different subjects.
WILL ROGERS

■ TIERING HOW-TO'S

You're now ready to use a tiered lesson with your class. You've laid the foundation for making students comfortable with doing different activities than their classmates. You've had discussions about how everyone is a unique learner and how everyone needs something different to succeed. You've been using flexible groups for a while. Now your students are skilled at moving in and out of various class arrangements, and you've become more comfortable with the movement and increased noise level of such groups activities (see Chapter 6). How can you make sure that the tiered lesson you are about to try will run smoothly?

Assigning Tasks

First, you have to make a few decisions about how to assign the tasks and announce students' assignments. As mentioned earlier, you may decide to let students choose their own tasks. In this case, print several copies of each task from the computer and glue them to index cards to make them more permanent. Let students select the task cards that reflect their activity choices. If you are assigning the tasks based on assessment data, you can simply write students' names in groups on the board or overhead and distribute task cards and assignments accordingly. For group-work activities let students form small groups of up to four members (larger groups tend to become less focused). Then, distribute different-colored folders or handouts containing several copies of the same task card for the group.

Grouping Students

Next, consider the types of groups in which students will work best and how you will maximize your time with students who need you the most. Keep in mind that the number of students working on a particular task will vary, and that it is up to you to decide whether each student will work on

online connection

Visit this Web site to find dozens of examples of lessons K–12 that are tiered by readiness, interest, and learning styles.

http://www.doe.state.in.us/exceptional/gt/tiered%5f curriculum/welcome.html

the task alone, with a partner, in triads, or in small groups. Note that your students' social abilities and group-work skills also will influence your choices. In my experience, students who have trouble focusing tend to remain more focused with one partner than in a larger group, while struggling students often benefit from peer input in small groups, usually with teacher assistance.

How might a whole-class configuration look? Depending on your class size, you might have one or two groups of four working on Task A (Tier I), six pairs working on Task B (Tier II), and one group of three working on Task C (Tier III). This would allow you to float between two groups of identified Tier I students, who will require more modeling, scaffolding, and direct instruction. Your paired students working on the Tier II task will be able to focus keenly and work without much intervention on your part; if partners have a question, they can ask for help from another pair nearby who are working on the same activity. You'll be able to check in on the group working on the most complex activity every once in a while; mostly they will be able to work independent of your help.

Fostering Independent Work Skills

To keep students from repeatedly coming to you with questions or distracting other students while you are working with other groups, I recommend that you invoke two surefire rules: "See three before me" and "Use six-inch voices." To implement the first rule, encourage students to ask for help from three others—a partner, or identified "student-helpers"—before coming to you. This will teach them to become more independent and it will foster collaborative skills as well. And for the second rule, explain that using voices that can be heard no further than six inches away will help all students to be able to focus on their own work and be less distracted. For more ideas on how to make tiering work, see Figure 7.3.

Self-Evaluation

At the end of the lesson, be sure to have students evaluate their group process. Have them ask each other: Did we stay on task? Did we follow the rules to "use six-inch voices" and "see three before me"? Did we engage in the anchor activity (early finisher's activity) if we completed the task early? What grade should we earn for class participation today? What goals do we need to set for the next group activity?

Figure 7.3

TIPS FOR TIERING

Lay the groundwork:

- Explain to students, "Fair is not equal. Fair is getting what you need."
- Lead a conversation about everyone needing different things to succeed in school.
- Have students create a visual representation, such as the Identifying My Strengths web, to help them see their strengths.
- Be clear about why one student's activity may differ from another's: "We're all different. Occasionally, we will be working on different activities. Each of us will be getting what we need."
- Use assessment data to determine placement of students in groups or allow students to choose which activity they want to try.
- Design similar activities, in which all students are focused on the same key understandings and skills, but at different levels of complexity, abstractness, and open-endedness.
- Design a similar-looking product for all of the groups.
- Start your planning with an activity for your on-level students. Then, create a more basic and a more complex version of that activity.
- Consider the time needed for each group's activities. Create similar time frames for completion (the same 15-, 20-, or 30-minute time segment).
- Have an "anchor activity" (a meaningful, independent activity) in place for groups/individuals who finish early.
- Teach students to "use six-inch voices" and "see three before me."
- Bring all groups together to share at the end of the tiered lesson.

Lesson Planning

Planning any good lesson takes patience and thoughtful design. Be flexible and persistent. Don't expect to master these strategies for differentiated planning right away. Work with colleagues to develop, try out, and evaluate your tiered lessons. Explore with them ways to improve the design and execution of your tiered lessons. To save time, plan a few tiered lessons that can be used more than once for reading, writing, speaking, and problem-solving activities. See Figure 7.4 for an example of a tiered math lesson that can be used over and over again with different graphs (and can be modified for use with charts, tables, maps, and documents). Figure 7.5 on page 140 illustrates a tiered research lesson that can be used many times throughout the year for any topic. As students become more comfortable at Tier I or Tier II levels, they can move to Tier II or Tier III activities the next time you use the lesson.

Planning and executing tiered lessons efficiently and effectively takes

Figure 7.4

A CLOSER LOOK AT TIERED LESSONS

Topic/Concept/Skills: Making and Analyzing Bar Graphs

- Use data to create a graph.
- Read and analyze graphs.

STUDENT READINESS	LEVEL OF TASK	BLOOM LEVEL
Struggles to understand concept/skill	**Tier I/Basic**	**Application/Analysis**

SAMPLE ACTIVITY (teacher-directed)

- Review the provided frequency table, titled "Our Favorite Desserts."
- Copy the provided graph onto grid paper. Include title, labels, and numbers on the scale.
- Complete the bar graph for each type of dessert. Make the length of the bar equal to the number of students who prefer that dessert.
- Complete cloze sentences to draw conclusions: *Most students prefer ____. More students prefer _____ than _____. Fewer students prefer _____ than _____. Fewest students prefer ____.*

Needs practice	**Tier II/On-grade**	**Analysis**

SAMPLE ACTIVITY

- Make a bar graph of the data in the frequency table showing the favorite pets of fourth graders in Mrs. Smith's class.
- Use a scale numbered by twos (0, 2, 4, 6, 8).
- Remember to title and label the graph.
- Answer guided questions about the graph to draw conclusions.

Has already mastered concept/skill; ready to extend learning	**Tier III/Advanced**	**Synthesis**

SAMPLE ACTIVITY

- Think of an idea for making a bar graph.
- Take a survey or collect data about the subject that interests you. Then, make a bar graph.
- Include a title and labels.
- List at least two conclusions drawn from the data.

practice because you must plan and implement the lesson with a number of elements in mind: targeting a key skill or objective to teach, matching tasks to student readiness, respecting differences among your students in interest and learning style, accounting for their social and emotional needs, and relying on good classroom management skills. Nevertheless, this instructional tool offers great promise in meeting the readiness needs of our diverse learners. Heterogeneous classrooms require differentiated instruction; tiered lessons should be at the core of that instruction.

Figure 7.5

A CLOSER LOOK AT TIERED LESSONS

Topic/Concept/Skills: Conducting Research

- Research any nonfiction topic (plants, animals, predators/prey, consumers/producers, weather, pollution, health habits, body systems, food pyramid, needs/wants, government, transportation, geography, occupations, etc.)
- Take notes as you read information.

STUDENT READINESS	LEVEL OF TASK	BLOOM LEVEL
Struggles to understand concept/skill	**Tier I/Basic**	**Application/Analysis**

SAMPLE ACTIVITY (teacher-directed)
- Teacher introduces key vocabulary terms.
- Students read with teacher/reading partners.
- Using guided questions, they discuss what they have read.
- Students complete provided graphic organizer or cloze sentences *(My animal lives__)* with terms from a word bank.

Needs practice	**Tier II/On-grade**	**Analysis**

SAMPLE ACTIVITY
- Students read on-grade-level material independently.
- Given a graphic organizer or outline with subtopics included, they take notes on details.

Has already mastered concept/skill; ready to extend learning	**Tier III/Advanced**	**Synthesis**

SAMPLE ACTIVITY
- Students create their own questions for research about the topic.
- Using several sources (text, nonfiction books, the Internet), students locate information.
- Students take notes in any format studied (outline, mapping, bullets, graphic organizer).

online connection

Visit the following Web site for information, resources, and strategies that can be used in a differentiated classroom.

http://teachereducation.wlu.edu/Differentiation.htm

Conclusion

I hope, as you work with the suggestions in this book, your commitment to differentiating instruction in your classroom deepens—even when the going gets tough. Please keep in mind that you may become frustrated from time to time. Things will be going along fine; then, you decide to try out a new strategy and, suddenly, everything seems to fall apart. For example, you might be comfortable working with small groups in which students are all doing the same activities. You decide to try out a tiered lesson in which you organize students into same-readiness groups and assign activities appropriate to each group's level of readiness. Suddenly, the noise level in your class escalates beyond control, several students want your attention at exactly the same moment, some students aren't sure what they should be doing, and a few students who finish early start to distract others.

When this happens, don't give up. It's normal—in fact, you can expect to face challenges with implementation whenever you try something new. Michael Fullan, an international authority on educational reform and one of the foremost thinkers on change theory, calls this phenomenon the "implementation dip" (Fullan, 2001). He reminds us that "change is a process, not an event." If things aren't working, you'll need to modify and adjust your plans. Don't hesitate to call a "time-out" from the activities in order to reconvene the entire class and solve some logistical challenges together. You may realize students need additional instructions. You may need to reorganize some of the groupings. You may need to remind students to follow certain procedures, including using quieter voices. By observing your students closely and assessing their progress, you will know when you need to adjust the task, the instructions, or the environment. Change takes time and creative problem-solving, but the end results—student engagement and achievement—are worth the effort.

A person who never made a mistake never tried anything new.
ALBERT EINSTEIN

With the strategies in this book to guide you in your planning, you need only the desire to make your instruction as effective as it can be. If you remain open and flexible, it is my belief that you'll be better at differentiating your instruction tomorrow than you are today, better next month than you are this month, better next year than you are this year. For a true professional, it's the journey of a lifetime. It's been a privilege to share my journey with you.

online connection

Visit this Washington and Lee University Teachers' Education Program Web site to find information, resources, strategies, and links for crafting your differentiated classroom:

http://teachereducation.wlu.edu/Differentiation.htm

Study Guide for Collegial Circles:

Differentiation in Action

This guide is designed to help you and your colleagues run a series of collegial circle discussions based on the underlying principles of differentiation found in this book. Laid out chapter by chapter, the questions posed will allow you to reflect upon your current practice, share with colleagues what is working and where you are experiencing difficulties, and consider what changes you might make in order to better meet the needs of your diverse learners.

I would suggest you spread your meetings apart by several weeks in order to go back into the classroom, observe and record present practice, and then try out new approaches several times. Keep in mind, change is messy, and it may take several weeks until you and your students are comfortable with a new approach or see positive results. Record and comment about any changes that you see taking place over time. Be sure to share this reflective journaling at each successive meeting.

You and your colleagues can take the role of circle leader on a rotating basis or one teacher can assume that role for the duration of your meetings. Be sure to present your proposal with this study guide to your district to learn if you and your colleagues can receive district credit for professional development. Although the required time for a collegial circle will vary based on the specific requirements of your district, for most districts, meeting time, reading time, and classroom-based action research is considered to be equivalent to a fifteen-hour course. Some groups may choose to meet before school; others may meet after school; still others may assign a chapter to be discussed at grade-level meetings.

When assigning a chapter to read, it is important to remind group members to set aside adequate time to read and reflect upon their current practice by journaling and responding to questions about the chapter. When members share the thoughts and feelings they've recorded, the group is likely to have a rich discussion that is grounded in their own experiences.

I hope you find this reflective practice with your colleagues to be enlightening and useful—for you and your students.

—Judy Dodge

online connection

You can find additional online resources to enhance learning in your classroom on my Web site,
www.judydodge.eboard.com.

TIPS FOR STRUCTURING A COLLEGIAL CIRCLE MEETING

PREPARING FOR THE MEETING

Each member contributes to the meeting by keeping a response journal.

- At home, use the response journal to reflect on your current practice and to consider new ideas from the reading. You might try one of the choice note-taking strategies suggested in Chapter 3 to help you record and comment on key ideas as you read.
- In your journal write all responses to the pre-reading questions in the study guide, as well as any during-reading and post-reading activities for which you need extra space. This record of your thoughts and ideas enables you to share your ideas with and get feedback from your colleagues at each session.
- During each session, make notes in your journal to synthesize what you are "coming to know" about differentiation. In this way, the journal serves as a reference guide for you throughout your circle study.

OPENING THE DISCUSSION

The group leader poses an open-ended question regarding the chapter previously assigned, such as:

- How does the information in this chapter inform your instruction?
- How can the ideas in this chapter help meet the needs of diverse learners?
- What questions do you have for the group to explore today as a result of your reading?
- (List the question and the group's responses on chart paper or a chalkboard.)

REFLECTING AND SHARING

Group members discuss new ideas and understandings about what they have read.

- Using sticky notes to find places that captured your attention during your reading, share with your colleagues ideas and concerns that you have regarding what you have read. Try to address the focus questions that have been posted by the group. Make sure the discussion includes examples from the book and examples from your own classroom.

DEVELOPING AN ACTION PLAN

Teachers decide what actions they can take to improve their practice.

- The leader can pose one of the following questions to the group and have teachers take five minutes to write down a plan in their journals:
- As a result of today's discussion about the reading, what changes do you plan to make with regard to your instruction?
- What strategies will you use to increase differentiation?
- Leave time for group members to share and give one another feedback or offer support. For example, consider which colleagues might work well together to develop or design a learning activity.

CLOSING THE CIRCLE

Tie up loose ends and plan for the next meeting.

- This might include summing up the key ideas in the chapter or tying up responses to focus questions. Before group members depart, set a reading goal for the next meeting. Remind group members to note any difference in student attitude or achievement that they notice over the next few weeks as a result of these changes.

INTRODUCTION (pages 6–9)

Before reading the book, reflect upon the following underlying principles presented on pages 6 and 7.

UNDERLYING PRINCIPLES OF EFFECTIVE INSTRUCTION IN A DIFFERENTIATED CLASSROOM

❒ Identify Principles that are established elements in your classroom by placing a ✔ in front of each one.

❒ Place a ⬆ next to Principles you want to explore and develop further for your classroom.

_____ Students do not all need to do the same work in the same way.

_____ Ongoing and frequent assessments serve as checks for understanding throughout the learning process.

_____ Multiple pathways for integrating information are used.

_____ Respect for all types of learners is apparent.

_____ Student-centered activities are encouraged.

_____ Reducing anxiety is a primary goal.

_____ Intrinsic motivation is fostered.

_____ Curriculum should be focused, relevant, thoughtful, and engaging.

_____ Lessons should be designed around "big ideas."

_____ Constructivist practices are frequently in evidence.

_____ Brain research informs instruction.

_____ Multiple intelligences and learning styles are addressed.

_____ Multi-modality approaches are enhanced by the frequent and varied use of visual tools and technology.

_____ Teaching styles and methodologies are frequently varied.

_____ Choice is often provided to appeal to students' talents, interests, and strengths.

_____ Flexible grouping is utilized.

_____ Scaffolding is provided for struggling and English language learners.

_____ Challenging options are provided for advanced learners.

_____ Opportunities are provided to help students develop skills as independent, self-directed learners.

❒ Scan this book and list 5 questions you hope will be answered:

- ______________________________
- ______________________________
- ______________________________
- ______________________________
- ______________________________

CHAPTER 1 (pages 10–26)

Celebrating the Unique Talents of All Learners

PRE-READING:

❒ In your journal:

- Brainstorm a list of ways your students differ from one another.
- List what you already do in your classroom to accommodate the needs of different learners.

DURING READING:

❒ Place sticky notes on strategies you want to try and ideas you want to remember.

❒ Consider the instructional approaches suggested in this chapter. At this point, which present the greatest challenge for you?

____

____

____

____

❒ List several ways you can accommodate students' different thinking styles, learning styles, and multiple intelligences preferences:

____

____

____

____

POST-READING:

❒ Share with your colleagues: Discuss the meaning of Gayle Gregory and Carolyn Chapman's quote reminding us that we must "bait" the hook with what the fish like, not what the fisherman likes. What instructional adjustments might you make to "bait the hook" for your students?

❒ In summary, what are the important ideas about teaching students with a range of strengths, needs, and differences that you want to keep in mind when addressing your students? (Consider posting some of these as reminders in a plan book or another place you often might look.)

- ______________________________________
- ______________________________________
- ______________________________________
- ______________________________________

CHAPTER 2 (pages 27–48)

Differentiating Instruction During the Three Phases of Learning

PRE-READING:

❐ Write a journal entry: Reflect on how you presently **introduce** a new topic or concept to your students. What types of learning activities do you have students **engage in during** the unit? When you **have completed** the topic, what do you have students do to reflect on or assess their learning?

DURING-READING:

❐ Place sticky notes on strategies you want to try and ideas you want to remember.

❐ List three new ideas you would like to try during each of the following phases of learning:

Before-learning:

- ____
- ____
- ____

During-learning:

- ____
- ____
- ____

Post-learning:

- ____
- ____
- ____

❐ Think of the students in your room who might enjoy creating an Artifact Box. Which needs might this activity address?

____

____

____

❐ Describe one or two ways you might adapt the Artifact Box activity for your students and curriculum:

____

____

❒ Explain how you might use Post-a-Points! and/or the Interactive Bookmark to improve reading in your classroom:

____

____

____

❒ Which Stop-and-Process activities do you want to try out with your class?

ACTIVITY	WHERE IT FITS IN MY DAY/LESSON

POST-READING:

❒ Using a copy of page 36, complete a Unit Planner for an upcoming unit.

❒ Make a list of between 10 and 15 items that you and/or your class could gather to create an Artifact Box for an upcoming unit.

Artifact Box for: ______________________________

- ______________________________
- ______________________________
- ______________________________
- ______________________________
- ______________________________
- ______________________________
- ______________________________
- ______________________________
- ______________________________
- ______________________________

CHAPTER 3 (pages 49–75)

Providing Choice During Instruction

PRE-READING:

❒ On a scale of 1 to 10, rate the level of your students' motivation to learn.

❒ What do you do presently to motivate students in your classroom?

DURING-READING:

❒ Place sticky notes on strategies you want to try and ideas you want to remember.

❒ Show the difference between extrinsic and intrinsic motivation by giving two contrasting examples of ways a teacher can motivate students:

❒ What conditions have you read about or noticed first-hand that tend to demotivate learners?

❒ Describe several ways you can foster intrinsic motivation in your classroom.

❒ Think of two students who seem unmotivated. What specific adjustments can you make to help motivate these students?

POST-READING:

❒ Choose at least one of the following:

- Create a list of **Choice Homework Options** that you can introduce easily and begin to use on a bi-weekly basis with your students.
- Choose one of the **Choice Note-Taking Options** and make a plan for its use.
- Create a **Choice Board** for an upcoming unit.

CHAPTER 4 (pages 76–87)

Differentiating Instruction Using Bloom's Taxonomy

PRE-READING:

❒ Write a journal entry: What do you remember about Bloom's Taxonomy? In what ways, if any, do you presently use the taxonomy in your instruction? Do you believe that all students can progress up the hierarchy in their thinking?

DURING-READING:

❒ Place sticky notes on strategies you want to try and ideas you want to remember.

❒ What is the difference between degree of difficulty and degree of complexity when designing learning tasks?

____

____

❒ Give an example of a recent activity you've assigned:

____

____

❒ How would you make it more difficult?

____

____

❒ Now, how could you make it more complex?

____

____

❒ Describe some ways you can use Bloom's Taxonomy to foster critical thinking in your classroom:

____

____

____

____

POST-READING:

❒ Design a set of Assessment in Bloom Activities at three levels of complexity. (Choose a topic and provide a choice of two activities for each level.)

CHAPTER 5 (pages 88–103)

Making Multiple Intelligences Work

PRE-READING:

❒ Write a journal entry: What do you know about Gardner's Multiple Intelligences theory? How do you presently integrate multiple intelligences into your curriculum? What are your feelings about using multiple intelligences when state and national assessments use standardized tests to assess skills in reading, math, and content areas?

DURING-READING:

❒ Place sticky notes on strategies you want to try and ideas you want to remember.

❒ Looking over the self-assessment on page 94, how would you describe yourself as a learner in terms of multiple intelligence preferences? (Use the space on the next page to give your response in writing, a picture, or a diagram.)

❒ Do your teaching methods tend to reflect these preferences? How can you stretch out of your comfort zone to accommodate students' preferences that may not be your own?

____

____

____

❒ Looking at page 95, choose two unique product ideas from each of the intelligences that you would like to try with your students.

Verbal-Linguistic

- ______________________
- ______________________

Spatial

- ______________________
- ______________________

Logical-Mathematical

- ______________________
- ______________________

Musical

- ______________________
- ______________________

Bodily-Kinesthetic

- ______________________
- ______________________

Naturalist

- ______________________
- ______________________

Intrapersonal

- ______________________
- ______________________

Interpersonal

- ______________________
- ______________________

❒ Why has the use of multiple intelligence–based activities in classrooms been questioned in many circles? What cautions should you take when using MI in your classroom?

POST-READING:

❒ Share and discuss with your colleagues: Has your understanding of/opinion about Multiple Intelligence theory changed since completing this chapter? What, if anything, has changed your mind?

❒ Using a copy of page 101, create a set of Gardner in Bloom Activities for your students. Choose your topic and then list the key understandings, skills, or focus questions essential to the unit. Let these elements guide you in designing the multiple intelligence–based activities at appropriate levels of complexity for your students.

HOW I LEARN BEST . . .

CHAPTER 6: (pages 104–126)

Maximizing Student Learning With Flexible Groupings

PRE-READING:

❒ Write a journal entry: To what extent are you comfortable using groups in your classroom? How do you feel about noise level during learning activities? What types of groups have you used? How often do you use groups? What concerns do you have regarding the use of group work?

DURING-READING:

❒ Place sticky notes on strategies you want to try and ideas you want to remember.

❒ What are the benefits to using flexible grouping over the predominant use of whole-class instruction?

____

____

❒ What are some of the problems you can expect when you first try a new grouping situation?

____

____

❒ What strategies have you read about or learned from colleagues that can help you minimize such problems?

____

____

❒ What are the benefits to each of the groupings explored in this chapter?

Individuals: ____

____

Partners: ____

____

Half-Class/Half-Class: ____

____

Small Groups (including needs-based, homogeneous, and heterogeneous groups):

____

____

Whole Class: ____

____

❒ List two or three new grouping strategies you'd like to try and one or two **learning activities** you might choose for each:

GROUP	LEARNING ACTIVITY

POST-READING:

❒ Share with your colleagues: Has your understanding of/opinion about using groups changed since completing this chapter? What, if anything, has changed your mind? What tips have you learned to make groups run more smoothly?

❒ Choose either a **Socratic Seminar** or a **Jigsaw activity** to design for your class. Write the topic, materials/text, and steps you will use for this activity. (Be sure to consider the amount of time students will need for each step.)

CHAPTER 7: (pages 127–140)

Tiering Lessons

PRE-READING:

❒ Write a journal entry: Imagine running a lesson where different students work at different levels of readiness on different activities. What problems do you anticipate/have you experienced with such a classroom design?

DURING-READING:

❒ Place sticky notes on strategies you want to try and ideas you want to remember.

❒ When does it make sense to tier a lesson?

❒ Name several ways you can provide scaffolding for a struggling learner:

❒ Name several ways you can challenge an advanced learner:

❒ How can you make tiering "invisible"?

❒ What data can you use to determine the groups?

POST-READING:

❒ Share with your colleagues: Have your feelings about tiering lessons changed since completing this chapter? What, if anything, has changed your mind? What tips have you learned to make tiered lessons run more smoothly? What concerns do you still have?

❒ Plan a tiered lesson for your class. Be sure to include two or three of these levels: **BASIC—ON-GRADE—ADVANCED**

FINAL REFLECTION:

❒ Have you found answers to the questions you posed before reading the text (page 144)?

❒ Do any original questions that you posed still remain unanswered? Where can you look for answers to these questions?

❒ How has your teaching changed as a result of this collegial circle?

❒ What differences do you note in students' learning and engagement as a result of this circle?

❒ What areas do you still want to focus on to continue enhancing differentiation in your classroom?

Works Cited

Anderson, L. W., & Krathwohl, D. R. (Eds.). (2001). *A taxonomy for learning, teaching, and assessing: A revision of Bloom's taxonomy of educational objectives.* New York: Longman.

Armbruster, B. B., Anderson, T. H., & Ostertag, J. (1987). Does text structure/summarization instruction facilitate learning from expository text? *Reading Research Quarterly, 22,* 3.

Armbruster, B. B., Anderson, T. H., & Ostertag, J. (1989). Teaching text structure to improve reading and writing. *Reading Teacher, 43,* 2.

Armstrong, T. (1998–2000). *Multiple intelligences.* Retrieved June 2005, www.thomasarmstrong.com/multiple_intelligences.htm.

Aronson, E. (2000). *Jigsaw classroom: tips on implementation.* Retrieved July 2005, www.jigsaw.org/tips.htm.

Aronson, E., Blaney, N., Stephan, C., Sikes, J., & Snapp, M. (1978). *The jigsaw classroom.* Beverly Hills, CA: Sage Publications.

Benjamin, A. (2003). *Differentiated instruction. A guide for elementary school teachers.* Larchmont, NY: Eye on Education.

Berk, L. E., & Winsler, A. (1995). *Scaffolding children's learning: Vygotsky and early childhood education.* Washington, DC: National Association for the Education of Young Children.

Billmeyer, R. (1996). *Teaching reading in the content areas: If not me, then who?* Aurora, CO: Mid-Continent Regional Laboratory.

Bloom, B. S. (1956). *Taxonomy of educational objectives: Handbook I. Cognitive Domain.* New York: David McKay.

Bloom, B. S. (1976). *Human characteristics and school learning.* New York: McGraw-Hill.

Bransford, J. D., Brown, A. L., & Cocking, R. (Eds.). (1999, 2000). *How people learn: Brain, mind, experience, and school.* Washington, DC: National Academy Press.

Bray, P., & Rogers, J. (1995). *Ideas in Bloom: Taxonomy-based activities for U.S. studies.* Portland, ME: J. Weston Walch.

Brimijoin, K., Marquissee, E., & Tomlinson, C. A. (2003). Using data to differentiate instruction. *Educational Leadership, 60,* 5.

Brooks, J. G., & Brooks, M. G. (1993, 1999). *In search of understanding: The case for constructivist classrooms.* Alexandria, VA: Association for Supervision and Curriculum Development [ASCD].

Beuhl, D. (1995). *Classroom strategies for interactive learning.* Schofield, WI: Wisconsin State Reading Association.

Bull, B. L., & Wittrock, M. C. (1973). Imagery in the learning of verbal definitions. *British Journal of Educational Psychology, 43,* 3.

Byrnes. J. (1996). *Cognitive development and learning in instructional contexts.* Boston: Allyn & Bacon.

Caldwell, J. S., & Ford, M. P. (2002) *Where have all the bluebirds gone? How to soar with flexible grouping.* Portsmouth, NH: Heinemannn.

Campbell, L. (1997). Variations on a theme: How teachers interpret MI theory. *Educational Leadership, 55,* 1.

Chapman, C., & King, R. (2005) *Differentiated assessment strategies: One tool doesn't fit all.* Thousand Oaks, CA: Corwin Press.

Ciardiello, A. V. (1998). Did you ask a good question today? Alternate cognitive and metacognitive strategies. *Journal of Adolescent and Adult Literacy, 42,* 3.

Contine, T. (1995). *Current brain research: Classroom applications—"Brain-friendly" teaching.* Kearney, NE: Educational Systems Associates.

Costa, A. L. (Ed.). (2001). A new taxonomy of educational objectives. In *Developing minds: A resource book for teaching thinking, 3rd ed.* Alexandria, VA: ASCD.

Costa, A. L. (Ed.). (2001). Visual tools for mapping minds. *Developing minds: A resource book for teaching thinking* (3rd. ed.). Alexandria, VA: ASCD.

Costa, A. & Kallick, B. (2000). *Discovering and exploring habits of mind.* Alexandria, VA: ASCD.

Countryman, J. (1992). *Writing to learn mathematics: Strategies that work, K–12.* Portsmouth, NH: Heinemann.

Curian, M. (2001). *Boys and girls learn differently! A guide for teachers and parents.* San Francisco: Jossey-Bass.

Daniels, H., & Bizar, M. (1998). *Methods that matter.* York, MA: Stenhouse.

Dodge, J. (1994). *The study skills handbook: More than 75 strategies for better learning.* New York: Scholastic.

Dunn, K., & Dunn, R. (1987). Dispelling outmoded beliefs about student learning. *Educational Leadership, 44,* 6.

Dunn, R. S., & Dunn, K. J. (1993). *Teaching secondary students through their individual learning styles: Practical approaches for grades 7-12.* Needham, MA: Allyn & Bacon.

Erwin, J. C. (2003). Giving students what they need. *Educational Leadership, 61,* 1.

Finney, S. (2000). *Keep the rest of the class reading and writing…while you teach small groups.* New York: Scholastic.

Foote, C. J., Vermette, P. J., & Battaglia, C. F. (2001). *Constructivist strategies: Meeting standards and engaging adolescent minds.* Larchmont, NY: Eye on Education.

Forsten, C., Grant, J., & Hollas, B. (2002). *Differentiated instruction: Different strategies for different learners.* Peterborough, NH: Crystal Springs Books.

Francis, R. C. (2003). *Why men won't ask for directions: The seductions of sociobiology.* Princeton, NJ: Princeton University Press.

Fullan, M. (2001). *Leading in a culture of change.* San Francisco: Jossey-Bass.

Gardner, H. (1983). *Frames of mind.* New York: Basic Books.

Gardner, H. (1993). *Multiple intelligences: The theory in practice.* New York: Basic Books.

Gardner, H. (2000). *Intelligence reframed: Multiple intelligences for the 21st Century.* New York: Basic Books.

Gardner, H. (2003). *Multiple intelligences after twenty years.* Paper presented at the meeting of the American Educational Research Association, Chicago, IL.

Gambrell, L., & Bales, R. (1986). Mental imagery and the comprehension-monitoring performance of fourth and fifth grade poor readers. *Reading Research Quarterly, 21*, 4.

Glasser, W. (1988). *Choice theory in the classroom.* New York: HarperPerennial.

Glasser, W. (1990). *The quality school: Managing students without coercion.* New York: HarperPerennial.

Glatthorn, A. (1999). *Performance standards and authentic learning.* Larchmont, NY: Eye on Education.

Goleman, D. (1995). *Emotional intelligence.* New York: Bantam.

Gregorc, A. F. (1982). *Inside styles: Beyond the basics.* Connecticut: Gregorc Associates.

Gregory, G. H., & Chapman, C. (2002). *Differentiated instruction strategies: One size doesn't fit all.* Thousand Oaks, CA: Corwin Press.

Gurian, M. (2001). *Boys and girls learn differently: A guide for teachers and parents.* San Francisco: Jossey-Bass.

Haggerty, P. (1992). *Readers' workshop: Real reading.* Toronto: Scholastic.

Heacox, D. (2002). *Differentiating instruction in the regular classroom: How to reach and teach all learners, grades 3–12.* Minneapolis, MN: Free Spirit Publishing.

Hirsch, E. D. (1996). *The schools we need: And why we don't have them.* New York: Doubleday.

Hobson, J. A. (1989). *Sleep.* New York: Scientific American Library.

Hyerle, D. (1996). *Visual tools for construction knowledge.* Alexandria, VA: ASCD.

Jensen, E. (1996). *Brain-based learning.* Del Mar, CA: Turning Point Publishing.

Jensen, E. (1998). *Teaching with the brain in mind.* Alexandria, VA: ASCD.

Johnson, B. (2003). *The student-centered classroom handbook: A guide to implementation.* Larchmont, NY: Eye on Education.

Johnson, D., Johnson, R., & Holubec, E. J. (1993). *Circles of learning: Cooperation in the classroom.* Edina, MN: Interaction Book Co.

Johnson, D., Johnson, R., & Holubec, E. J. (1998). *Advanced cooperative learning.* Edina, MN: Interaction Book Co.

Jones, B. F., Palinscar, A. S., Ogle, D. S., & Carr, E. G. (1987). *Strategic teaching and learning: Cognitive instruction in the content areas.* Alexandria, VA: ASCD.

Kagan, S. (1995). *Cooperative learning: Theory, research and practice, 2nd ed.* Needham, MA: Allyn & Bacon.

Kagan, S. & Kagan, M. (1994). The structural approach: Six keys to cooperative learning. In S. Sharan (Ed.). *Handbook of cooperative learning methods.* Westport, CT: Greenwood Press.

Keene, E. L. & Zimmerman, S. (1997). *Mosaic of thought: Teaching comprehension in a reader's workshop.* Portsmouth, NH: Heinemann.

King, A. (1990). Reciprocal peer questioning: A strategy for teaching students how to learn through lectures. *The Clearing House, 64*, 131–135.

Lazear, D. (2004). *OutSmart yourself! 16 proven multiple intelligence strategies for becoming smarter than you think you are.* Chicago, IL: New Dimensions Press/IPG.

Levine, M. (2002). *A mind at a time.* New York: Simon and Schuster.

Lyman, F. (1988) Cueing thinking in the classroom: The promise of theory-embedded tools. *Educational Leadership, 45*, 7.

Lyman, F. (1981). The responsive classroom discussion: The inclusion of all students. *Mainstreaming Digest.* College Park, MD: University of Maryland.

Manzo, A. V. (1969a). Improving reading comprehension through reciprocal questioning (Doctoral dissertation, Syracuse University, Syracuse, NY, 1968). *Dissertation Abstracts International, 30*, 5344A.

Manzo, A. V. (1969b). The request procedure. *Journal of Reading, 13*, 123–126.

Manzo, A. V. (1990). *Content area reading: A heuristic approach.* Columbus, OH: Merrill.

Manzo, A. V. & Manzo, U. C. (1995). *Teaching children to be literate: A reflective approach.* Fort Worth, TX: Harcourt Brace College.

Marzano, R. J. (2003). *What works in schools: Translating research into action.* Alexandria, VA: ASCD.

Marzano, R. J., Pickering, D. J., & Pollock, J. E. (2001). *Classroom instruction that works: Research-based strategies for increasing student achievement.* Alexandria, VA: ASCD.

McLaughlin, M. & Vogt, M. (2000). *Creativity and innovation in content-area teaching.* Norwood, MA: Christopher-Gordon.

Means, B., Chelemer, C., & Knapp, M. (Eds.). (1991). *Teaching advanced skills to at-risk learners: Views from research and practice.* San Francisco: Jossey-Bass.

Miller. G. A. (1983, December 25). Varieties of Intelligence; Frames of Mind: The Theory of Multiple Intelligence. *New York Times Book Review*, p. 5.

Moline, S. (1995). *I see what you mean: Children at work with visual information.* York, ME: Stenhouse.

Neuthall, G. (1999). The way students learn: Acquiring knowledge from an integrated science and social studies unit. *Elementary School Journal, 99*, 4.

Neuthall, G., & Alton-Lee, A. (1995). Assessing classroom learning: How students use their knowledge and experience to answer classroom achievement test questions in science and social studies. *American Educational Research Journal, 32*, 1.

Nicholson-Nelson, K. (1998). *Developing students' multiple intelligences: Hundreds of practical ideas easily integrated into your lessons and activities.* New York: Scholastic.

Paivio, A. (1969). Mental imagery in associative learning and memory. *Psychological Review, 76*, 241–263.

Paivio, A. (1971). *Imagery and verbal processing.* New York: Holt, Rinehart, & Winston.

Paivio, A. (1990). *Mental representations: A dual coding approach.* New York: Oxford University Press.

Pauk, W. (1997). *How to study in college, 6th ed.* Boston: Houghton Mifflin.

Renzulli, J., Leppien, J. H., & Hays, T. S. (2000). *The multiple menu model: A practical guide for developing differentiated curriculum.* Mansfield Center, CT. Creative Learning Press.

Reutzel, D. R. (1999). Organizing literacy instruction: Effective grouping strategies and organizational plans. In L. B. Gambrell et al. (Eds.), *Best practices in literacy instruction.* New York: The Guilford Press.

Rowe, M. B. (1972). *Wait-time and rewards as instructional variables: Their influence in language, logic, and fate control.* Paper presented at the National Association for Research in Science Teaching, Chicago. (ERIC Document Reproduction Service No. ED 061 103).

Schelechty, P. (1997). *Inventing better schools: An action plan for educational reform.* San Francisco: Jossey-Bass.

Silver, D. (2003). *Drumming to the beat of a different marcher: Finding the rhythm for teaching a differentiated classroom.* Nashville, TN: Incentive Publications.

Silver, H. F., Hanson, J. R., Strong, R. W., & Schwartz, P. B. (1980). *Teaching styles and strategies.* Trenton, NJ: Thoughtful Education Press.

Silver, H. F., Strong, R. W., & Perini, M. J. (2000). *So each may learn: Integrating learning styles and multiple intelligences.* Alexandria, VA: ASCD.

Silver, H. F., Strong, R. W, & Perini, M. J. (2001). *Tools for promoting active, in-depth learning.* Trenton, NJ: Thoughtful Education Press.

Singer, H. (1978). Active comprehension: From answering to asking questions. *Reading Teacher, 31*, 8.

Sousa, David A. (2001). *How the brain learns.* Thousand Oaks, CA: Corwin Press.

Sprenger, M. (2003). *Differentiation through learning styles and memory.* Thousand Oaks, CA: Corwin Press.

Stahl, R. J. (1994). Using "Think-Time" and "Wait-Time" Skillfully in the Classroom. ED370885.

Strong, R., Hanson, J. R., & Silver, H. (1995). *Questioning styles and strategies, 2nd ed.* Woodbridge, NJ: Thoughtful Education Press.

Strong, R., Thomas, E., Perini, M., & Silver, H. (2004). Creating a differentiated mathematics classroom. *Educational Leadership, 61*, 5.

Stronge, J. H. (2002). *Qualities of effective teachers.* Alexandria, VA: ASCD.

Sylwester, R. (1990). Expanding the range, dividing the task: Educating the human brain in an electronic society. *Educational Leadership, 48*, 2.

Sylwester, R. (1995). *A celebration of neurons: An educator's guide to the human brain.* Alexandria, VA: ASCD.

Tharp, R. G., & Gallimore, R. (1988). *Rousing minds to life.* New York: Cambridge University Press.

Tomlinson, C. A. (1999). *The differentiated classroom: Responding to the needs of all learners.* Alexandria, VA: ASCD.

Tomlinson, C. A. (2000). Reconcilable differences? Standards-based teaching and differentiation. *Educational Leadership, 51*, 1.

Tomlinson, C. A. (2001). *How to differentiate instruction in mixed-ability classrooms* (2nd ed.). Alexandria, VA: ASCD.

Tomlinson, C. A. (2004). Differentiation in diverse settings. *The School Administrator, 61*, 7.

Tomlinson, C. A. & Cunningham Edison, C. (2003). *Differentiation in Practice: A resource guide for differentiating curriculum—grades 5–9.* Alexandria, VA: ASCD.

Tompkins, G. E. (1998). *50 literacy strategies.* Upper Saddle River, NJ: Merrill.

Tompkins, G. E. (1994). *Teaching writing: Balancing process and produce, 2nd ed.* New York: MacMillan.

Vacca, R. T. & Valla, J. L. (1996). *Content area reading, 5th ed.* New York: HarperCollins.

Vygotsky, L. S. (1978). *Mind in society: The development of higher mental processes.* M. Cole, V. John-Steiner, S. Scribner, & E. Souberman (Eds.). Cambridge, MA: Harvard University.

Vygotsky, L. (1986). *Thought and language, revised ed.* Kozulin, A. (Ed.). Cambridge, MA: MIT Press.

Wiggins, G., & McTighe, J. (1998). *Understanding by design.* Alexandria, VA: Association for Supervision and Curriculum Development.

Wiggins, G., & McTighe, J. (1998). *Understanding by design.* Alexandria, VA: ASCD.

Willingham, D. T. (2005). How we learn: Ask the cognitive scientist. *American Federation of Teachers.* Summer: 31–36.

Wolfe, P. (2001). *Brain matters.* Alexandria, VA: ASCD.

Winebrenner, S. (2001). *Teaching gifted kids in the regular classroom, revised edition.* Minneapolis, MN: Free Spirit Publishing.

Wrubel, R. M. (2002). *Great grouping strategies: Dozens of ways to flexibly group your students for maximum learning across the curriculum.* New York: Scholastic.

Wycoff, J. (1991). *Mindmapping: Your personal guide to exploring creativity and problem-solving.* New York: Berkley Books.

Index